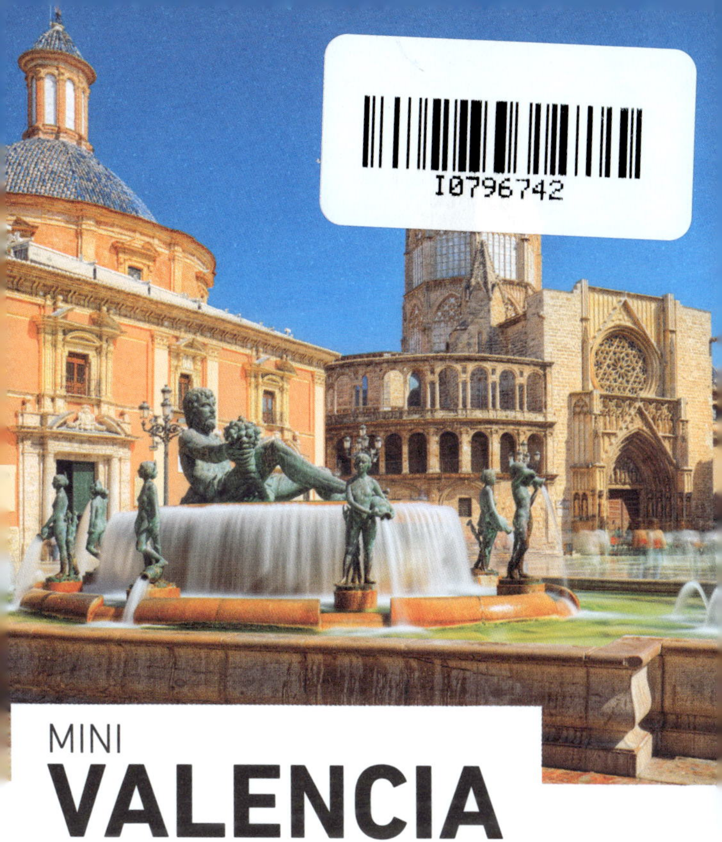

MINI
VALENCIA

YOUR TAILOR-MADE TRIP STARTS HERE

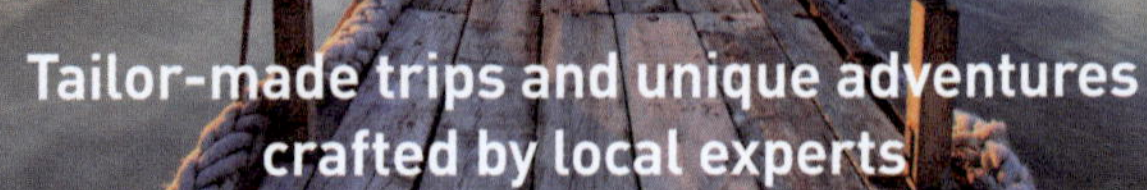

Tailor-made trips and unique adventures crafted by local experts

HOW ROUGHGUIDES.COM/TRIPS WORKS

STEP 1

Pick your dream destination, tell us what you want and submit an enquiry.

STEP 2

Fill in a short form to tell your local expert about you dream trip and preferences

STEP 3

Our local expert will craft your tailor-made itinerary. You'll be able to tweak and refine it until you're completely satisfied.

STEP 4

Book online with ease, pack your bags and enjoy the trip! Our local expert will be on hand 24/7 while you're on the road.

PLAN AND BOOK YOUR TRIP AT ROUGHGUIDES.COM/TRIPS

How to download your Free eBook

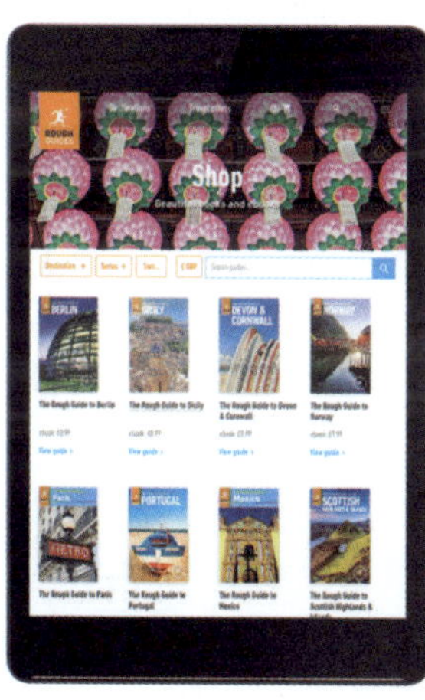

1. Visit **www.roughguides.com/free-ebook** or scan the **QR code** opposite

2. Enter the code **valencia468**

3. Follow the simple step-by-step instructions

For troubleshooting contact: mail@roughguides.com

Contents

Introduction

As Spain's third city after Madrid and Barcelona, in terms of population, Valencia enjoys this top billing in more ways than one. The city is graced with a glorious natural setting, an agreeable climate and a laid-back vibe; not to mention boasting an arguably better standard of living than the top two to boot.

Natural splendour

Founded by the Romans over two thousand years ago, Valencia stands on a shallow scoop of a bay half-way down the Mediterranean coast. Curiously, however, it wasn't founded on the shoreline but a little way inland. Valencia, it always used to be said, 'had its back to the sea'; with its commercial and fishing port kept at an avenue's length from the city centre, so as not to distract from the enjoyment of exploring its handsome monuments and

WHAT'S NEW

The most recent sight to open in Valencia is the Centro de Arte Hortensia Herrero (see page 48), a stunning contemporary art gallery in a restored mansion. You'll find several famous names, including Sean Scully, Olafur Eliasson and David Hockney, in its bright white galleries. The Iglesia de San Nicolás (see page 43), known as the 'Sistine Chapel of Valencia' for its extraordinary vault paintings, has been transformed into an immersive audiovisual attraction, the Light of San Nicolás. In the city centre there are two splendid new viewpoints to complement the iconic Miguelete: the *Atenea Sky* rooftop restaurant and the belltower of the Iglesia de Santa Catalina (see page 35). The latest addition to the City of Arts and Sciences is the CaixaForum cultural centre (see page 65), an eye-catching arched building that looks like the ridged back of a blue dinosaur. The city's network of cycle tracks continues to expand, taking pedal-power far out into the *huerta*, the surrounding farmland.

pretty squares and gardens but with the added benefit, naturally, of being right by the sea.

The city grew up on the right bank of the River Turia, which flows off the high plateau in the centre of Spain into the Mediterranean. However, following a disastrous flood in 1957 its course was diverted along an artificial channel around the outer suburbs instead – you can still walk along the banks of what was once the Turia but today the dry bed is a long ribbon of parks and playing fields, crisscrossed by an attractive mix of historic and modern bridges.

Mercat Central

So, while the city is not quite on the sea and the river has changed its course, it remains the hub of a prodigiously fertile plain known as the *huerta* – an intricate mesh of market gardens, orange groves and rice fields. The harvest wealth from this fertile land has always been the foundation for Valencia's prosperity and appeal, and this is duly acknowledged. Everywhere you look, motifs of fruits, flowers and country life are glorified in stone and stained glass, and most strikingly in the brilliance of the city's famous multicoloured ceramic tiles.

Valencia transformed

Surprisingly, for all its natural advantages, Valencia has been slow to lure in foreign visitors. This is not for want of attractive qualities.

Monuments it has aplenty – especially glorious Gothic buildings dating from its fifteenth-century heyday, when it was one of the most prosperous mercantile cities in Europe. Museums and art galleries are also in abundance, as well as gardens, elegant public squares and grand avenues lined by palms and billowing fig trees. All this in a compact, easily walkable city centre that was largely bypassed by tourists through ignorance rather than intent.

Not so anymore. In recent years, the world has woken up to what Valencia has to offer just as Valencia itself has begun to realise its true tourist potential. The city is in the throes of regeneration. The once run-down medieval quarter of the Barrio del Carmen has been transformed into a trendy enclave, its once-arid riverbed now home to one of the boldest architectural initiatives in Europe, the City of Arts and Sciences (see page 63). After dark, the district comes alive as crowds gather in its bars and restaurants.

Everywhere you look, Valencia is busy reimagining itself – laying out new avenues and metro lines, remodelling the old and

WHEN TO GO

The summer months are peak tourist season in Valencia – best avoided if you don't like crowds and heat. August is Spain's holiday month, and the city's beaches are at their busiest then. To beat the hordes but still hope for good weather, visit Valencia in spring (excepting Easter weekend). Temperatures should be ideal for sightseeing, biking and city strolls. Early autumn is also a good option, when it is usually still warm, but most visitors have gone home. Winter has its advantages: November to March is rarely cold, and you can expect pleasant enough days that you can enjoy a drink outdoors; however, pack a jumper as the evenings can be nippy. Above all, unless you are expressly looking for action – and willing to pay for it – avoid the Fallas festival in March when hotels are booked up way in advance and prices exorbitant. Whichever time of year you plump for, it's wise to bring a raincoat or umbrella as there are often sporadic showers and occasional heavy downpours.

building new hotels, bridges and shopping centres. Its port was given a much-needed facelift to receive the America's Cup and even served as a Formula 1 circuit for several years.

Living the good life

What is really striking about contemporary Valencia is not that it is bristling with new developments, but that it is learning to show off and share the simple, good things in life that Valencians have long appreciated. And indeed, it is this '*buena vida*' that is turning out to be its most marketable commodity.

Proof of this begins in the central market (one of the biggest in Europe), which receives the huge quantities of fresh produce that pour into the city daily from farms and fishing fleets. Valencian cuisine makes straightforward use of this abundance in a range of rice dishes, including Spain's national dish, paella. Invented in the *huerta* and imitated the world over,

Colourful houses in Port Saplaya

NOTES

Valencia is a city of over 824,000 people. It is both the capital of a province of the same name and of an autonomous region, the Comunidad Valenciana, which stretches from the borders of Catalonia to the southern reaches of the Costa Blanca. Both city and region are bilingual with Valencian – a softer form of Catalan – enjoying equal status with Spanish (Castilian).

Valencia at night

SUSTAINABLE TRAVEL

Valencia's city centre is small enough to make walking everywhere a plausible option. To visit outlying sights, rent a bike or other pedal-powered vehicle. Alternatively, the public transport network – metro, tram and bus – is so good that you should only need a taxi if you are out very late at night. In your accommodation, use the energy-guzzling air conditioning sparingly and switch it off when you head out. Traditional neighbourhood bars are preferable to fast-food restaurants because they generally rely on less packaging and prepared food, and use locally sourced ingredients. Naturally, everywhere you go, pick up your litter and make the effort to look for recycling bins, which are plentiful. When visiting La Albufera and its coast, the Dehesa, stick to designated footpaths to avoid damaging the local flora.

a well-prepared paella is both colourful and appetising – it looks as good as it tastes. In restaurants all over the city you can eat the real thing – perhaps even cooked in the traditional way over a wood fire, outdoors among friends.

Then there's the city's nightlife, the so-called 'Moon of Valencia'. In such a benign climate it's easy to go out late and stay out late, with or without kids in tow. The extrovert parade around the well-known zones of prolific *bars* (in the Spanish sense of the word – loud, stripped-down, night-time bars with standing room only), while those in search of a less raucous time can cherry-pick from a decent range of more sedate and sophisticated bars and cafés.

And as if the energetic after-dark scene wasn't enough, Valencia punctuates the year with some of Spain's most showy *fiestas*, in particular, the unmissable Fallas in March – a riotous week of non-stop commotion that culminates with the burning of giant comic sculptures in narrow streets and teeming squares.

NOTES

In 2003 the world's most prestigious yachting regatta, the America's Cup, was won by a European team for the first time in 152 years. The Swiss winners chose to host the 32nd America's Cup in Valencia in 2007 thanks to its excellent wind and wave conditions. Some of the facilities built for the occasion, notably the Edificio Veles e Vents (see page 69), remain as quayside landmarks.

City and country

If you tire of the urban pace, there are sandy beaches to relax on; quieter towns in the Valencian hinterland to explore; and fresh countryside air to breathe in. Country and city are united by the brilliant Mediterranean light and, in spring, the sweet scent of orange blossom, or *azahar*. It's no cliché to say that it is a place where the senses are constantly stimulated.

10 Things not to miss

1 **MIGUELETE TOWER**
Climb the distinctive belltower of the cathedral. See page 38.

2 **BARRIO DEL CARMEN**
The most fashionable part of the city, day and night. See page 43.

3 **LAS FALLAS**
A spectacular festival where sculpture meets fire. See page 91.

4 **TORRES DE SERRANOS**
A reminder of the medieval city. See page 57.

5 **MERCADO CENTRAL**
The best place to sample local food. See page 46.

6 **MUSEO DE BELLAS ARTES**
A stunning collection featuring many of the great masters. See page 58.

7 **LA LONJA**
A silk merchants' market dating from the fifteenth century. See page 47.

8 **LA ALBUFERA**
One of Spain's most important bird habitats. See page 76.

9 **CIUTAT DE LES ARTS I LES CIÈNCIES**
Valencia's twenty-first-century architectural showcase, with lots to see and do. See page 63.

10 **MUSEO NACIONAL DE CERÁMICA**
A visual feast inside and out. See page 49.

A perfect day in Valencia

9AM

Breakfast. Start the day in the splendidly tiled *Horchateria Santa Catalina* (Plaza Santa Catalina 6). Its speciality is *horchata*, a sweet, milky drink made with tiger nuts, usually drunk later in the day. A better choice is a *café con leche* with an *ensaimada* (a sweet bun) on the side.

10AM

Old Valencia. Take a tour of the historic core of the city. Start at the Mercado Central (see page 46), a glorious Art Nouveau market hall where you'll see Valencia at its liveliest, and then cross the road to the graceful Gothic hall of La Lonja de la Seda (see page 47).

11AM

Catedral. From here, wander through the atmospheric old streets of the Barrio del Carmen towards the Catedral (see page 36). For those with a head for heights, and able for it, climb the 207 spiral steps to its belfry, the Miguelete, for an unbeatable panoramic view over the city's rooftops.

NOON

To the seaside. Walk up the road from the Plaza del Virgen, behind the cathedral, to the riverbank near the Torres del Serrano. Cross the pedestrian bridge to reach the tram station. Take line 4 to the port (see page 69) and stroll around the quayside before meandering along the Paseo Marítimo at the head of the beach.

2PM

Lunchtime. Enjoy Valencia's signature dish of paella over a long, lazy seaside lunch (ordered in advance) at *La Pepica*, or any of the other restaurants along the Paseo Neptuno.

4PM

Cultural complex. From Marítim station near the port, catch metro line 5 to Alameda and walk up the riverbank to the extraordinary gleaming white buildings of the City of Arts and Sciences (see page 63). Looking like something out of a sci-fi movie, the cultural complex is a sight to behold. The Oceanogràfic aquarium is the best of the attractions here to visit (see page 65).

7PM

Time for tapas. Head back to the city centre and join the throngs converging at the city's tapas bars for an evening drink and bite to eat. One of the best in town is *La Pilareta* (Moro Zeit 13), which has been operating since 1917 and is renowned for its excellent mussels.

10PM

Dinner and drinks. Indulge in a gourmet meal at swanky *Ricard Camarena Restaurant* (Avda. Burjassot 54), followed by a nightcap in one of the many bars of the Barrio del Carmen (see page 43). This is where to sample Valencia's vibrant nightlife – though things don't really get going until after midnight and the party continues well into the early hours.

Valencia by bike

10AM

Cycle the old riverbed. Pick up a rental bike from the city centre (see page 31) and join this route at the most convenient point. From the Plaza Porta del Mar, near the tourist information office, take the cycle lane down Calle de la Justicia. Cross the main road at the end of the bridge, descend into the now-dry riverbed and pick up the track heading 'downstream'. You'll pass beneath a string of bridges and skirt the supine figure of Gulliver (see page 62) before reaching the City of Arts and Sciences (see page 63).

11AM

The esplanades. When you're ready to continue, leave the riverbed just beyond the Science Museum. From the gigantic roundabout at Plaza de las Falleras Mayores, join the cycle lane along Calle Menorca. Head right onto Avenida del Puerto to reach the port (see page 69). Skirt the harbourfront to the left (north), turn down Paseo de Neptuno and keep on the track that joins the Paseo Marítimo along the beach (see page 69).

NOON

Beach time. You'll probably want to spend time at the beach: to have a swim, eat an ice cream, or simply watch the world go by. If you're feeling energetic, you could cycle all the way down the Paseo Marítimo. Otherwise, potter around and linger where you please.

2PM

Lunchtime. A string of restaurants along Malvarrosa beach will furnish you with a choice of tapas or a full meal. Afterwards, you might want to find a shady palm tree for a siesta.

4PM

Cabanyal. Cycle back up the Paseo Marítimo until just before you reach *Las Arenas* hotel. Turn right down the cycle track tracing Calle Pescadores. Cross Calle del Dr Lluch and Calle de la Reina with care and continue in the same direction through the narrow streets of the Cabanyal fishing quarter (see page 72). Perhaps pause to explore the generations-old shops and neighbourhood bars, checking out the ornate tiled facades and pasted-painted houses.

5PM

Los Viveros. At the busy junction by El Cabanyal railway station, pick your way across the road to the start of Avenida de Blasco Ibañez, where a gently winding cycle track leads all the way down this wide thoroughfare. You'll reach Los Viveros, the city's largest gardens (see page 58), studded with fountains, pergolas and sculptures galore. Turn left across the sixteenth-century Puente de Real, skirt Plaza Tetuán and you'll be back at your starting point in time to freshen up for the evening.

Valencia for art lovers

10AM

Museo de Bellas Artes. While this route attempts to squeeze in as many galleries as possible in a day, you may choose to linger in one and skip another. Note that most galleries are closed on Monday and also Sunday afternoons. After breakfast in the city centre, cross the riverbed to the Museo de Bellas Artes (see page 58) for an overview of Valencia's art history. Check out the stunning collection of altarpieces, then head to the upper floors to peruse the nineteenth- and early-twentieth-century art by famous local artists, including Sorolla.

NOON

Casa Museo de José Benlliure. Cross back over the river and turn right to follow the bank 'upstream', passing the fourteenth-century Torres de Serranos (see page 57), to reach the Casa Museo de José Benlliure, dedicated to the life and work of the renowned early-twentieth-century artist (see page 56).

1PM

Institut Valencià d'Art Modern. Continue along the riverbank in the same direction and turn left at the next main intersection. Here, Valencia's museum of modern art, the Institut Valencià d'Art Modern (IVAM; see page 55), always has something surprising and thought-provoking to offer.

3PM

Lunchtime. Either eat in the Mediterranean-style restaurant in IVAM, or you can easily find somewhere else to dine nearby.

4PM

Iglesia de San Nicolás. Leaving IVAM, head down Calle Guilhem de Castro until you reach the Torres de Quart, one of the old city gates. Turn left up Calle de Quart, cross Plaza Tossal and set off on Calle Caballeros. Swerve right down an alleyway to see the glorious eighteenth-century frescoes of the Iglesia de San Nicolás (see page 43), now presented as a sound and light show called the 'Light of San Nicolás'.

6PM

Centro de Arte Hortensia Herrero. Pedal along Calle Caballeros into Plaza del Virgen. Turn right and skirt the cathedral to reach Plaza de la Reina, then head down Calle de la Mar to the Centro de Arte Hortensia Herrero (www.cahh.es). Here, you can browse a stunning collection of contemporary art creatively displayed in a beautiful old mansion.

8PM

Downtime. Once you've had your fill of art riches, it's time to relax. Be sure to start the evening with a glass of Agua de Valencia in the artistic cocktail bar, *Café Madrid* (Calle de l'Abadia de Sant Martí 10), before heading in search of dinner.

History

Although, as innumerable archaeological finds attest, the uplands of eastern Spain have been continuously inhabited since the Stone Age, the city of Valencia itself is of comparatively recent origin. It was founded, as Valentia, in 138 BC by the Roman consul Decimus Junius Brutus to accommodate legionnaires who had served in the victorious campaign against the Lusitanians in the west of the Iberian Peninsula. He chose as a site an island in the River Turia roughly equidistant between the two important Roman cities of Tarraco (Tarragona) and Cartago Nova (Cartagena). The place was marshy and inhospitable but easily defended against attacks by local groups of Celtiberians.

As Valentia grew and thrived, its early tents and huts were replaced by mud and stone houses protected by a wall. But all this was destroyed by Pompey in 75 BC as he waged civil war against Sertorius. The settlement was abandoned for almost fifty years before being reoccupied. This time it expanded more securely, acquiring a forum, baths, circus, river port and systematic water supply. When the Roman Empire began to decline, however, Valentia spiralled with it. Its public buildings fell into disuse, and entire suburbs were deserted.

In the fourth century, a Christian community was established around the memory of St Vincent who was tortured and martyred here in 304. Gradually, as the Church grew in power and importance, the ecclesiastical authorities assumed the governance of the city. However, in the mid-sixth century Valencia came under the sway of the Visigoths, former allies of Rome.

NOTES

According to legend, when El Cid died in 1099, the Moors were besieging Valencia but the sight of his body being led out of the city propped up on a horse was enough to panic the attackers. They fled the city.

Muslim Valencia

El Cid, Spain's national hero

In 711 Muslim invaders from North Africa – the Moors – defeated the Visigoths and in the following years overran Spain. There is little documentary evidence from Valencia (Balansiya at that time), but it is known that the emir of Cordoba, Abd al-Rahman, sacked the city in 778 to quash a rebellion and that his son Abd allah al-Balansi built a palace in what is now the suburb of Russafa. Islam became the dominant religion – although Christianity and Judaism were tolerated – and Arabic the language of official transactions and daily life. When the caliphate of Cordoba disintegrated in 1010, Balansiya became the capital of an independent kingdom or *taifa*.

At the end of the eleventh century the Christian warrior Rodrigo Díaz de Vivar, better known as El Cid, captured Balansiya and briefly ruled it as his own fief. Shortly after his death it was seized by an Arab army and was to remain a Muslim city for over 130 years.

Islam was not, however, to retain its foothold in Europe forever, and the Christian reconquerors of Spain made steady progress south. As they approached Balansiya, the city's defences were strengthened, but on 9 October 1238, the city fell to Jaime (James) I, king of Catalonia and Aragón, bringing it into the mainstream of European civilisation. Under Jaime I, Muslim possessions were shared among Christian barons, and the city became the capital

LEGACY OF THE MOORS

Although the Moors ruled Valencia effectively for over four centuries, few monuments have survived from that time; but they did leave something of much more lasting significance, the *huerta*. This intensely cultivated alluvial plain, which takes over where the suburbs end, is still irrigated by an ingenious system of dams and channels created by Moorish farmers to feed the prodigiously productive orchards and market gardens. Here they cultivated the crops they had brought with them to Spain: rice, sugar cane, cotton, saffron, oranges, lemons and mulberry trees (the food plant of silkworms).

of a new kingdom of Valencia, under the aegis of the crown of Aragón. Valencia was granted its own *furs*: laws guaranteeing its right to self-governance with its own institutions and currency.

The Middle Ages

Although the fourteenth century was a traumatic time for Valencia, punctuated by rebellion, war and the Black Death, it was also a period of growth as immigrants arrived in large numbers to work in the textile industry. By the end of the century, Valencia was entering its golden age, a period of prosperity built on enterprise and trade. As one of the most important ports on the Mediterranean – indeed, one of the most important cities in Europe – it became the most populous city in Spain, a cosmopolitan, mercantile and financial metropolis. Its docks would be busy unloading Genoese and Venetian ships, which had arrived laden with Italian fabrics, gold and enslaved Africans, and which would depart packed with wool, leather, ceramics and the produce of the *huerta*. The most emblematic building surviving from this time is the silk exchange of La Lonja, looking more like a temple than a trading floor.

The flow of wealth sparked a simultaneous flowering in the arts and learning: some of the first print shops in Spain were set up and the university was founded. This was also the time of two influential Valencian writers: the poet Ausias March and Joanot Martorell, the knight-author of *Tirant lo Blanc*, a novel of chivalry praised by Cervantes as 'the best book of its kind in the world'.

Despite economic and cultural prosperity, however, social, economic, religious and political tensions were simmering and these exploded into revolt in 1519 when the *germanías* – brotherhoods of artisans, peasants, the petty bourgeoisie and low-ranking clergy – rose up against the nobility and seized control of the city. Civil war rampaged across the kingdom, and the revolt was quelled by a repressive Spanish monarchy anxious to assert its centralising authority on the regions of a newly unified Spain.

Map of the Valencian region, 1640

Expulsion of the Moors

There was, however, a further crisis on the cards as the Counter-Reformation took hold in Spain. Although many Muslims had fled Valencia when it had been reconquered, many had stayed and continued their way of life under Christian rule, accepting nominal conversion to Christianity. The Moriscos, as they were known, made up a sizeable proportion of Valencia's population. Some, however, observed the tenets of Islam in secret, wore Muslim costume and spoke Arabic. Royal decrees issued between 1525 and 1526 sought to prohibit these lingering vestiges of Muslim Spain but, as the nobles of Valencia were economically dependent on the craft skills and labour of the Moriscos, they protected them from the Inquisition and for decades the orders were not effectively enforced. When, at last, the Moors were expelled from Spain by Felipe (Philip) III in 1609, Valencia is estimated to have lost almost a third of its workforce, leaving some villages without inhabitants and depriving key industries – notably that of silk-making – of their most skilled workers.

Expulsion of the Moors, Vincente Lopéz Portaña

Just over a century later, Valencia again became disastrously embroiled in national politics. The death of King Carlos III without an heir divided the country – and Europe – between supporters of the Bourbon pretender Felipe V and Archduke Charles of Austria, who arrived in Spain in 1707 to claim the crown. Valencia sided with the latter but when Charles's supporters were defeated at the Battle of Almansa on 25 April 1707, the victorious Felipe took revenge with a decree abolishing the autonomous status of Valencia as enshrined centuries before in the *furs*. A garrison of soldiers was installed in the city, and a mostly Castilian aristocracy took over its administration.

Industrialisation

The nineteenth century was also a turbulent time for Spain, beginning with invasion. In the aftermath of the French Revolution the country was plunged into the Peninsular War (known in Spain as the War of Independence), and Valencia was twice besieged and occupied for a year and a half by the troops of Napoleon under General Suchet. Following the departure of French forces, the liberals of Spain enjoyed a brief ascendancy before Fernando (Ferdinand) VII disembarked at Valencia, declaring the restoration of the absolutist Bourbon monarchy and ushering in a period of repression. Fernando's death sparked a crisis of succession and for seven years the country was ruled by the regent María Cristina until she was forced out of power, fleeing Valencia into exile in 1840. The struggle between liberalism and conservatism, royalists and republicans, limped on for the rest of the century.

Notwithstanding events in Madrid, the Valencian economy grew and matured during the nineteenth century. The city rapidly industrialised. As steam engines gradually began to power factories, increasing output, so wage-labour replaced traditional artisan activities. Silk production, introduced a thousand years before by the Moors, fell into decline to make way for modern industries such as metallurgy, ceramics, chemicals and furniture-making – sucking in vast numbers of immigrants from the countryside. Between 1800 and 1900 the city's population soared from 50,000

NOTES

Spearheaded by writer Constanti Llomber and journalist Teodoro Llorente, the *Renaixença* (Renaissance) cultural movement arose in the 1870s to promote the literary worth of the Valencian language and the values of Valencian identity.

to 215,000. In the ensuing pressure to build houses, roads and railways, it was decided, in 1865, to demolish the 4.5km (3 miles) of medieval city walls, creating work for potentially rebellious redundant silk-factory workers. This was also a time of renaissance for Valencian regional identity, and the Valencian language and traditions regained respectability lost in centuries of centralisation.

The Civil War

For all its economic growth, Spain began the twentieth century with its political problems still unresolved. The installation of the Second Republic in 1931 brought hopes of greater democracy, land reform, and the recognition of regional identities in Spain, but opinion was fast polarising between revolution and reaction. Things came to a head on 17 July 1936 when military plotters led by General Francisco Franco launched a revolt against the elected government, plunging the country into civil war. Franco's Nationalist uprising failed in large parts of the country, including Valencia, which sided with the beleaguered Republic.

For a time, it seemed that either side might prevail. Early on, the Nationalist forces threatened to take Madrid, and in November 1936 the government moved to Valencia, which became the de-facto capital of Spain. The parliament was housed in the city hall and La Lonja, and the government in Benicarló Palace. As the Nationalists advanced after the fall of Catalonia, refugees poured into the city, which clung on until the very end. Bombed, shelled from the sea and besieged, its fate seemed inevitable. On 30 March

1939, the day before the end of hostilities, Valencia was entered by Nationalist forces under General Aranda.

The post-war period

In the early years of Franco's regime, the whole of Spain suffered from shortages, hunger and economic paralysis, but Valencia, which had sided against the dictator, was also subjected to a centralising, homogenising force even more severe than that of the absolutist monarchs of old. It was deprived of political autonomy, and use of the Valencian language was prohibited. As if things weren't bad enough, in 1957 the River Turia broke its banks and caused serious flooding. The river was subsequently directed into a new, artificial course around the outside of the urban area.

Gradually, as Spain recovered economically during the 1960s, Valencia's standard of living rose and new blocks of flats were constructed and motorways built, eating up the shrinking farmland of the *huerta*.

Modern Valencia

Franco's death in 1975 made way for a transition to democracy. On 23 February 1981 new-won freedoms were threatened by a coup d'etat launched by officers of the Guardia Civil.

Painting of the martyrs from Valencia, Ernesto García Lledó

Aftermath of the flood in Catarroja, 2024

Ultimately, the coup failed, but not before General Milans del Bosch ordered his tanks down the Gran Via of Valencia to point their guns at the headquarters of the Socialist Party.

The restoration of democracy returned a large measure of autonomy to Spain's regions. The use of the Valencian language was now not only permitted but encouraged: it is taught in schools and given equal status to Spanish (Castilian) in all official documents.

Devolution also triggered a recovery of regional pride, and since the mid-1980s the city has been in the throes of regeneration. The old quarter of El Carmen, for a long time seedy, has been gentrified. The dry bed of the River Turia has been transformed into a ribbon of gardens and sports facilities. A modern metro and tramway have been laid out, and the long-neglected beachfront treated to a broad *paseo* (promenade) lined with palm trees. But the many new buildings have been eclipsed by the opening of the City of Arts and Sciences, an ambitious cultural complex worthy of any sophisticated European city. The whole neighbourhood of El Cabanyal is also being given a thorough revamp after years of being threatened with destruction, while a new 56km 'cycling ring' around the city is the finishing touch to an already-extensive network of bike lanes.

Chronology

138 BC Valentia founded as colony for Roman legionnaires.

75 BC Valentia destroyed by Pompey in his civil war against Sertorius.

AD 304 St Vincent the Deacon is martyred in Valentia.

711 Moorish conquest of Spain.

778 Abd al-Rahman, emir of Cordoba, attacks and sacks the city.

1010 Balansiya becomes capital of a kingdom or *taifa*.

1094 El Cid seizes Balansiya. In 1102 it falls again into Muslim hands.

1238 The city is conquered by Jaime I of Aragón-Catalonia.

1262 Foundation stone of Valencia cathedral laid.

1348 Black Death.

1474 Valencia becomes part of the Spanish state by the marriage of Fernando II of Aragón and Isabel of Castile.

1499 La Lonja completed; university founded.

1609 Expulsion of Moors from Spain by Felipe III.

1702–14 War of the Spanish Succession.

1707 Felipe V wins Battle of Almansa. Valencia loses its *furs* (privileges).

1812–13 Napoleonic occupation under Suchet.

1936–9 Spanish Civil War.

1957 River Turia causes serious flooding.

1982 Valencia is granted autonomous statute.

2004 City of Arts and Sciences completed.

2007 America's Cup held in Valencia.

2008 The Valencia Street Circuit is built around the harbourside for the Formula One European Grand Prix.

2011 Francisco Camps steps down as premier following allegations of involvement in the Gürtel corruption case.

2015 Joan Ribó becomes mayor, succeeding the late Rita Barberá.

2023 A plan to drive an avenue through the picturesque Cabanyal quarter is abandoned. María José Catalá is elected mayor.

2024 A freak DANA cold-drop storm strikes in October, causing torrential rain and fatal flash flooding in towns southwest of the city.

Santiago Calatrava's stunning Palau de les Arts

Places

The city centre, bordered to the north by the dry bed of the River Turia, to the south by the railway station and to the east and west by broad avenues, is compact enough to walk around. Most of the major sights are contained within this area, except for a few scattered along, or on, the far bank of the Turia. To travel further afield there is an efficient bus and metro system that connects with a modern tramway to the beach. Another popular option is to hire a bike and take advantage of the city's flat terrain and network of cycle lanes.

City centre

Highlights

- **Plaza del Ayuntamiento**, see page 32
- **Plaza de la Reina and Plaza Redonda**, see page 34
- **The Cathedral**, see page 36
- **Plaza de la Virgen**, see page 40
- **Barrio del Carmen**, see page 42
- **The Market and La Lonja**, see page 45
- **The Centro de Arte Hortensia Herrero and the Museo de Cerámica**, see page 48
- **The university and El Patriarca**, see page 51

Whether or not you arrive by train, a good place to begin a tour of Valencia is the mainline railway station, the **Estación del Norte**. Built between 1907 and 1917 in a style inspired by Austrian Art Nouveau, it is far more than a mere transit terminal; this is a celebration of the agricultural abundance of Valencia. Its twin white towers are hung with bunches of sculpted oranges. Inside there is yet more citrus fruit, this time in stained glass. In the foyer and cafeteria, meanwhile, are ceramic murals depicting the life and crops of the *huerta*, the farmland around Valencia.

Over the road from the station is the nineteenth-century **Plaza de Toros**, four floors of 384 identical brick arches making a structure reminiscent of a Roman amphitheatre and with seats for 17,000 people. The bullfights here during the Fallas festival in March constitute the first of the official season. Next to it, in Pasaje Doctor Serra, is one of the oldest bullfighting museums in Spain, the **Museo Taurino** (charge; www.museotaurinovalencia.es).

Plaza del Ayuntamiento

From the station it is a short walk to the triangular main square, the **Plaza del Ayuntamiento**. Laid out in the 1920s, it has had four names during its short history. During Franco's time it was known in his honour as the Plaza del Caudillo but after his death, the citizens of Valencia were quick to remove the title and the statue of their defunct leader mounted proudly on a horse.

Presiding over the square, the **Ayuntamiento** ❶, or city hall (free; www.valencia.es), is an ornate palace of municipal authority that is essentially two buildings in one. First came a convent-like girls' school, founded in the nineteenth century by the archbishop of Valencia. The later addition, a dignified civic palace, is distinguished by its twin domes on the corner, a clock tower and a large ceremonial balcony plonked in the middle. At the tower's base stand a statue of the city's coat of arms, and four statues

THE CITY'S SYMBOL

In front of the city hall, at the base of the clock tower, is a statue of the city's coat of arms held by two naked females and surmounted by a bat (*rat penat* in Valencian, meaning 'winged rat') – the symbol of Valencia since the thirteenth century. In 1238, while Jaime I of Aragón was going about the business of conquering Moorish-held Valencia, a bat is supposed to have perched on his helmet. This was seen as an omen of good fortune and, ever since then, the creature has retained its significance to the city.

The town hall in the Plaza del Ayuntamiento

representing Prudence, Fortitude, Justice and Temperance. Peek inside the city hall to see a handsome marble staircase, ornate council chamber and reception room, and municipal museum.

Across the square is the **post office** building, with sculpted angels, representing the speed of modern communications, hovering over its facade. The letterboxes at ground level, down a side street, take the form of snarling bronze lions' heads.

On the same side of the square is the **Ateneo Mercantil** cultural centre. Head around the back and take the lift to the eighth-floor *Atenea Sky* restaurant (Calle de Moratín 12; free on weekdays; www.ateneasky.com) on the rooftop for one of the best views of the city.

If the centre of the square between these buildings seems devoid of interest except for its flower stalls, it's because it is kept as a public space for *fiestas*, in particular the Fallas (see page 91), when the largest of the city's combustible works of art is installed here. Before and during the festival, the square is also used as the setting for a *mascletà*, a peculiarly Valencian tradition of letting off firecrackers in synch in broad daylight with the aim not to make pretty visual effects but instead to create a deafening but – or so Valencians think – harmonious din.

Plaza de la Reina and Plaza Redonda

Continue out of the square via its apex, walking in the same direction in which you arrived, and you will join Calle San Vicente Mártir. This leads you towards the second most important square, the Plaza de la Reina. On your right you pass the Pasaje Ripalda, a shopping gallery with a glass roof. Take the alley on your left before you reach Plaza de la Reina and you will step into the charming **Plaza Redonda** ❷ ('Round Square'). This caprice of mid-nineteenth-century urban development, inaccessible to cars, is known affectionately by the locals as El Clot (The Hole). A small ring of stalls, arranged around the fountain in the middle, specialises in haberdashery, ceramics and work clothes.

Plaza Redonda

You can easily get lost exploring the maze of streets beyond the Plaza Redonda, but for now it is best to retrace your steps up the alley and continue into the

WHERE TO SHOOT THE BEST PICTURES

City centre views. There are three high points from which to capture a picture of the rooftops or looking down on the streets: the Miguelete (see page 38), the belltower of the Catedral; the belltower of the Iglesia de Santa Catalina (see page 35) and the *Atenea Sky* restaurant (see page 33), which overlooks the Plaza del Ayuntamiento.

The houses of the seafront. The Cabanyal (see page 72) and Malvarrosa quarters are dotted with traditional houses decorated in colourful tiles. Wait for the sun to hit your subject before taking your shot.

The City of Arts and Sciences. The futuristic buildings of this cultural complex (see page 63) in the old riverbed create striking images from several angles.

The Albufera and the rice fields. To take nature shots, particularly birds, head for the freshwater lake (see page 76) south of the city. The mosaic of paddy fields can produce some evocative images at sunset.

Oranges galore. The Mercado Central (see page 46) is brimming with colourful produce, good for close-ups. It is courtesy to ask permission from stallholders and perhaps buy a little something to say thank you.

Plaza de la Reina (formerly known as Plaza Zaragoza). As a taster before visiting the cathedral, which lies ahead of you, it is worth visiting the **Iglesia de Santa Catalina** ❸, impossible to miss because of its distinctive Baroque belltower built on a hexagonal plan. The church proper inside is not Baroque at all, but a pure and soothing Gothic. For a small fee, technically a donation, you can climb the spiral staircase to the top of the tower to take in the view. Near the entrance to the church, is one of Valencia's oldest *horchaterías* (see page 111): **Santa Catalina** (www.horchateriasantacatalina.com), with tiled decorations, glass display cases and marble tables, it's worth stopping in for a coffee and a sweet treat.

VIA AUGUSTA

Once Spain had been brought fully under Roman control, the Emperor Augustus (27 BC–AD 14) ordered a road to be built down the east coast, linking the Pyrenees and Cádiz. Named the Via Augusta after the emperor, it extended 1500km (930 miles) and was the longest Roman road in the Iberian Peninsula. Although it was primarily intended to enable troop movements, it also facilitated trade. Its route runs through Sagunt to Valencia where it passes through the Plaza de la Reina in the centre of the city.

The cathedral

The top side of the Plaza de la Virgen is formed by Valencia's magnificent **Catedral** ❹ (charge; www.catedraldevalencia.es), with its octagonal belltower, El Miguelete, rising above it. The foundation stone for the building was laid in 1262 on the site of a mosque, and although it was begun in the prevailing Romanesque style the majority of it is Gothic. You wouldn't think so, however, on the approach from the square because the doorway before you, the **Puerta de Hierros**, is unrestrained Baroque, the work of Konrad Rudolf, a German pupil of Bernini. Although this is the main facade, it looks cramped and uncomfortable because it had to be superimposed on a pre-existing building, with the immovable El Miguelete taking up much of the space.

Before stepping inside, skirt around the building to the right to see the Romanesque **Puerta del Palau**, which gives on to the Plaza del Palacio del Arzobispal. This has a pleasingly understated decoration: the fourteen small heads beneath the cornice are said to represent seven men and their wives who came from Lerida to repopulate Valencia after the Christians had reconquered it from the Moors.

Once inside the cathedral you can fully appreciate its basic Gothic structure. It is lit by an elegant *cimborrio*, an octagonal, two-storey lantern pierced by windows of delicate tracery, the sunlight filtered through panes of alabaster.

The altar, however, is an elaborate configuration of Renaissance and Baroque art, the altarpiece itself is the work of two artists heavily influenced by Leonardo da Vinci. One grisly point of interest behind the altar is the brown and shrivelled mummified forearm of St Vincent the Deacon, co-patron of the city, who was martyred in Valencia in 304.

Altogether more beguiling is the cathedral's most famous relic, what is claimed to be the **Holy Grail**, the cup that Jesus Christ drank out of at the Last Supper. The small, dark red agate cup, which in the fourteenth century was set in a gold framework

The cathedral's Gothic nave

VALENCIA'S HOLY GRAIL

Like Turin's shroud, the purported Holy Grail in Valencia's cathedral has been the subject of a great deal of speculation. In 1960, a professor of archaeology at Zaragoza University dismantled and examined the cup and proclaimed it to be of a date prior to Jesus Christ and made in a workshop of the now Middle East; but there is no evidence connecting it directly to New Testament events.

According to legend it was taken from Jerusalem to Rome by Saint Peter and there used by popes to celebrate mass. When the Emperor Valerian persecuted the Church and tried to confiscate its treasures, San Lorenzo – the first deacon of the Church – dispatched the grail to Huesca, in the Pyrenean foothills, for safety, three days before being martyred for his faith. It now made its appearance in historical documents. During the Muslim conquest of the Iberian Peninsula, the grail was kept in the remote monastery of San Juan de la Peña.

In 1437 it arrived in Valencia where it has been ever since, except during the Napoleonic occupation of Spain when it was smuggled out for safe-keeping.

studded with jewels, is on display in a rather gloomy chapel, formerly a chapterhouse, beneath a roof of stellar vaulting sprouting from coloured bosses.

The Chapel of the Holy Grail gives access to the **cathedral museum** (https://museocatedralvalencia.com), which houses a handful of treasures, including some of the original polychrome statues, two paintings by Goya, other paintings by Juan de Juanes and a giant monstrance which is carted through the streets of Valencia during the procession of Corpus Christi.

Before leaving the cathedral, climb the octagonal belltower of the **Miguelete**, or Micalet in Valencian (extra charge), which demands the giddying ascent of a spiral staircase of over two hundred steps to a 50m (160ft) -high terrace above the city streets below. The tower owes its name to its date of consecration:

29 September 1418, the feast day of the archangel St Michael, Miguelete being the affectionately diminutive form of his name.

From the tower, peels rang across the city in the late Middle Ages announcing the times to open and close the city gates. The bellcote crowning the edifice today is, however, a later addition.

Outside the cathedral

Leave the cathedral by the door opposite the main entrance, the **Puerta de los Apóstoles**, a triumph of fourteenth-century Gothic sculpture attributed to Nicolás de Ancona. Glance behind to admire the veritable crowd of Biblical characters gathered around the door, including fourteen angels, sixteen saints, eighteen prophets and, to the sides of the door, the apostles standing on triangular pillars and sheltered by tabernacles. All these statues were originally coloured and kept repainted until at least 1522, when they began to be badly worn by the elements. The worst eroded were withdrawn in modern times and have been replaced with copies.

The Miguelete

Every Thursday at noon this doorway becomes the setting for what is perhaps the most extraordinary court of law anywhere in the world. It is here that the **Water Court** (Tribunal de las Aguas) meets in public and in the open air to decide disputes between farmers over the use of irrigation water in the *huerta* around the city. The eight judges dressed in black smocks – all farmers themselves, elected by their peers – represent the different networks of water channels. Hearings are instant and oral (in Valencian): no records are taken; no appeal is possible: and no business is put off until another session. The court has met in this way weekly, with scarcely a break since 1239. When there is no debate, the affair can be over as the clock strikes midday – so arrive promptly if you want to watch the spectacle. If it rains, the Water Court meets in an adjacent building.

Plaza de la Virgen

The Puerta de los Apóstoles opens into the **Plaza de la Virgen** (built on top of the Roman forum), now a car-free place to mill around or sit in a pavement café and watch life go by. In the middle of the square is a fountain representing the god Triton, personifying the River Turia, surrounded by eight figures with pitchers pouring water, representing the principal irrigation channels feeding the *huerta*.

The cathedral shares this square with two other impressive buildings. Beside the Puerta de los Apóstoles is what looks almost like a lost section of the Colosseum. This is an arcaded gallery belonging to the cathedral known as **Els Balconets de la Seu**, which serves as a dais from which church dignitaries can watch processions and other events taking place in the plaza. The most spectacular of these is La Ofrenda, part of the Fallas festival, when a huge copy of the statue of Valencia's patroness,

NOTES

Many streets and squares in Valencia have two names, one in the Valencian language and one in Spanish (Castilian). Also, somewhat confusingly, some squares have changed their names within living memory, but locals will refer to them by their former name – be prepared.

The fountain on Plaza de la Virgen

the Virgen de los Desamparados (the Virgin of the Forsaken or Helpless), is made out of bunches of flowers brought by a lengthy procession of people dressed in traditional costume.

The actual statue of the Virgin is of a more modest size and form, although obscured by the wig, rich clothes and jewels that lavishly adorn her. It is kept on display above the altar in the church dedicated to her, the seventeenth-century **Basílica de la Virgen de los Desamparados** (free; https://basilicadesamparados.org). The sculpture is poised on a swivel mechanism so that it can be brought to face the nave of the church or a small chapel intended for more intimate communion with the faithful.

Behind the church, through the arch formed by the bridge to the cathedral, is the Plaza de la Almoina. Just off this is a smaller square, mostly covered in glass, beneath which are the ruins of the original Roman settlement of Valentia. They can be visited via the **Centre Arqueologic de L'Almoina** (charge). Two other sights near here are the **Museo de la Ciudad** (charge), housed in the former Palacio del Marqués de Campo, and **El Almudín** ❺ (charge), a thirteenth- to fourteenth-century granary which once supplied the city with wheat and is now used to house exhibitions. Down an adjacent street, Calle del Almirante, meanwhile, is the only piece of Moorish architecture still standing in the city, the **Baños del Almirante** (the Admiral's Baths; charge; currently under renovation with no set date for reopening).

Return to the Plaza de la Virgen, where you will see before you the seat of the Valencian regional government, the **Palau de la Generalitat** ❻ (free; visits by appointment). It looks old enough to be a fusion of Renaissance and Gothic, but only one tower is authentic – the other is a copy added in 1952.

Another important institution is housed in an old palace to your right, on the pedestrianised Calle Navellos, which leads north towards the Torres de Serranos and the river. This is the **Cortes Valencianas** (free; visits by appointment; www.cortsvalencianes.es), the regional parliament of the Comunidad Valenciana. It occupies the much-extended Palacio de Benicarló, which became the home of the Republican government in the Civil War after its exile from Madrid until the final victory of Franco's forces.

NOTES

The statue of Valencia's patroness Virgin is nicknamed the Geperudeta, the 'Little Hunchback', because of a curve in its back. The story goes that the statue assumed this form through use in the funeral rites of outcasts such as executed criminals. The sculpture would be laid on the corpse, her head resting on a cushion, a position that caused her 'curvature of the spine'.

Barrio del Carmen

The street that runs beside the Palau de la Generalitat is

Calle Caballeros, the principal axis of Valencia's oldest and most atmospheric quarter, the **Barrio del Carmen** ❼, a tangle of narrow, twisting streets and alleys which suddenly open out into unsuspected, quiet little squares. Once rundown, it has been successfully regenerated, preserving the buildings' original architectural details and allowing the district's unique character to shine through. At night it is transformed into one of Valencia's favourite nightlife haunts.

Barrio del Carmen, a favourite nightlife haunt

Calle Caballeros is lined with mansions of more or less Gothic pedigree, mostly built around inner patios – often concealed behind street doors large enough to admit carriages when opened but forbidding enough to keep the riffraff out when shut. One such mansion has been converted into a museum of toy soldiers, L'Iber (charge; www.museoliber.org).

An alley to the left of Caballeros leads to the Iglesia de San Nicolás, which has been dubbed the 'Sistine Chapel of Valencia' for its glorious ceiling frescos. The church is run as a themed attraction called the Light of San Nicolás (charge; www.sannicolasvalencia.com, a sound and light show explaining the church and its art.

A right turn on the other side of Caballeros, on to Calle Salinas, connects to the **Portal de Valldigna**, once part of the 2m (6.5ft) -thick ramparts built by Valencia's Muslim rulers. In the

Imposing Torres de Quart

seventeenth century, two houses on either side of the street were joined together over the top of the gate.

At the end of Caballeros is the Plaza del Tossal. Here, a section of the Moorish-era wall, together with a watchtower, can be seen in the **Galería del Tossal** (free). It is believed to be part of the al-Hanax gate, one of the city's five entrance points built between 1021 and 1061 when Valencia was capital of a Muslim kingdom.

A short walk beyond the Plaza del Tossal, down Calle de Quart, brings you to the edge of the Barrio del Carmen, marked by the **Torres de Quart** ❽, one of the old city gates. This was built between 1441 and 1460, using Naples' Castel Nuovo as a model. When the walls fell into disuse, the gate was turned into a women's prison. The holes that stud the outside walls are said to have been made by projectiles fired by the French during their siege of Valencia in 1808 and left unrepaired as a memorial to the resilience of the citizens.

The market and La Lonja

South of the Barrio del Carmen, down Calle Bolsería from Plaza del Tossal, you come to three very different buildings sharing the triangular **Plaza del Mercado**, where those deemed heretics by the Inquisition were burned at the stake.

Church of the St John

The **Iglesia de los Santos Juanes** ❾ began life as a Gothic structure, built on the site of a mosque. It was badly damaged by fires in the sixteenth century and had to be almost totally rebuilt over the following two centuries. Only the nave and a large blank disc at the west end, which was to have been a rose window, nod to the church's Gothic origins. The frescoes of the Apocalypse on the vaults by Antonio Palomino are worth checking out, as are the statues of the Twelve Tribes of Israel, sculpted by Jacobo Bertessi.

The main facade, forming an odd juxtaposition with the other two buildings on the square, is unusual for having a terrace jutting out from its base, which was used as a platform from which dignitaries could watch public spectacles. Beneath, the basement chambers with doors onto the street are known as **les covetes de Sant Joan** (St John's caves). At the top of the facade is a clocktower with figures of the two St Johns to whom the church is dedicated.

NOTES

The spire of the Iglesia de los Santos Juanes used to be crowned by a weather-vane of a bird which, according to tradition, was used as a distraction by poor parents who wanted to abandon their children: they would point to the bird and, when the child was looking up, slip away into the crowd.

Mercado Central

Adjacent to the church, the **Mercado Central** ⑩ (free; www.mercadocentralvalencia.es) is the principal market of the city – and one of the biggest in Europe – housed in a handsome Art-Nouveau building with wrought-iron vaults and a central dome. Designed for the everyday business of buying and selling, it nevertheless has delightful ornamental touches in ceramic, brick and stained glass – most notably the red and yellow stripes of Valencia's flag, the *senyera*. There are around seven hundred stalls, best browsed mid-morning when the market bustles with people calling out their orders in Valencian and stuffing shopping baskets and trolleys with fruit and vegetables. If you are not venturing out into the

Mercado Central

huerta, where oranges are sold by growers on the roadsides, buy these citrus delights here. You'll also find herbs, spices, dried fruit and nuts; one vendor even specialises in ostrich eggs and meat. A separate part of the market is for fish and seafood.

Outside, if you are in need of a pick-me-up, buy a portion of freshly fried *churros* – essentially long, thin doughnut sticks – or a takeaway serving of paella. Look out for the stall near the entrance that sells paella pans in a variety of sizes with gas rings to match, together with all the necessary cooking implements.

La Lonja

Across the road from the market is Valencia's favourite building, a true temple to commerce. **La Lonja de la Seda** ⓫ (charge), originally used for trading in silk and later as a general commodities exchange, is one of Europe's finest examples of civil Gothic architecture. It was modelled on a similar building in Palma de Mallorca and built between 1483 and 1498.

The exterior is lavishly decorated in carved stone with tracery, filigree, *ajimez* windows (divided into two lights by slender columns) and spiky crenellations beneath which gargoyles leap out. If you look closely at street level, you can see a glimpse of the more playful side of the craftspeople responsible: among the figures scored into the stone is one revealing his naked buttocks.

The building is divided into three parts by a central tower, which contains a chapel and a prison once used for merchants who defaulted on their debts. The section to the left was occupied by two institutions: the **Consulado del Mar**, a regulatory body that oversaw maritime trade, and the **Taula de Canvis**, the city's first banking body, which was largely responsible for financing the construction of La Lonja.

To the right of the tower, the **Transactions Hall**, divided into three naves, is the building's most graceful space. The high ceiling is held aloft by eight elegantly spiralling columns that

Interior of La Lonja, the fifteenth-century silk merchants' market

sprout at the top into stellar vaulting. An inscription running round the chamber reads, 'I am a famous house which took fifteen years to build. See how fine a thing commerce can be when its words are not deceitful, when it keeps its oaths and does not practise usury. The merchant who lives in such a way will have riches and enjoy eternal life.'

Behind La Lonja is a warren of narrow streets and squares dotted with small shops. With luck you should emerge beneath the tower of the Iglesia de Santa Catalina, at the corner of the Plaza de la Reina, ready to visit a very different part of the city centre.

The Centro de Arte Hortensia Herrero and the Museo de Cerámica

From the bottom of Plaza de la Reina, the ruler-straight **Calle de la Paz** leads towards the modern shopping zone of the city centre. Running parallel, a few steps to the north, the Calle de la Mar shelters the impressive **Centro de Arte Hortensia Herrero** (charge, buy your entrance ticket from the show across the street; www.cahh.es). A renovated Baroque mansion dating to the seventeenth century, the Palacio de Valeriola now houses an important private collection of contemporary art, including paintings and sculptures. Highlights include Sean Scully's transformation of the palace's chapel (first floor); Olafur Eliasson's colourful *Tunnel for Unfolding Time* (second floor); and two rooms dedicated to David Hockney (second floor). In the basement, exhibits trace the history and renovation of the building, plus there's a display of substantial ruins from Valencia's Roman circus.

Behind the art gallery is Valencia's oldest church, the **Iglesia de San Juan del Hospital** (free but charge for guided tour; www.sanjuandelhospital.es) which has the remains of a medieval cemetery and intriguing thirteenth-century wall paintings in one side chapel. A sliding stone slab in the small courtyard opens on to a surviving part of the central spine of the city's Roman circus.

Cross Calle de la Paz and take Calle Marqués de Dos Aguas to reach Spain's national ceramics museum, the **Museo Nacional de Cerámica González Martí** ⓬ (charge; www.cultura.gob.es/mnceramica/home.html), set within an eighteenth-century extravaganza of coloured plaster, the Churrigueresque (an extreme Spanish form of Baroque) mansion of the Marquis of Dos Aguas. The doorway is particularly striking. It is a dripping fantasy in alabaster designed by Hipólito Rovira and created by the sculptor Ignacio Vergara. Ostensibly, it is a portrait of the **Virgen del Rosario** but below it

The Museo Nacional de Cerámica González Martí

becomes a pun on the marquis' surname, Two Waters. On either side of the door two semi-nude male figures recline, while below them water representing the two rivers of Valencia – the Turia and Júcar – flows from twin pitchers. Around the figures runs a voluptuous mass of vegetation.

Beyond the portal, the museum doesn't disappoint. It is an eclectic delight of all things old and dazzling – even if you can't get excited about pottery and porcelain, you are likely to find something among the collections to fascinate you. To begin with there are the rooms of the mansion itself, with their spiralling gold columns hung with grapes, cherubs and pink plaster cornices. The most striking single exhibit, perhaps, is the marquis' Cinderella-style formal **Carriage of the Nymphs**, another Rovira/Vergara over-indulgence in excessive ornamentation. Other intriguing items include canopied beds and various items of furniture, a collection of Ex-Libris bookplates, old posters, photographs, books, sketches, engravings, caricatures, jewellery, silver and ephemera galore to do with celebrated Valencians.

The ceramics museum proper has some five thousand pieces beginning with prehistoric, Greek and Roman specimens, passing through Oriental designs, and ending with creations by Picasso. The core of it was amassed by Manuel González Marti, discoverer of potteries that flourished in the Middle Ages near Valencia. The outstanding treasures are medieval pieces produced in ceramic-making towns near Valencia – Paterna, Manises and at the Royal Factory in Alcora – which are vibrant in greens, blacks and blues, often with metallic sheens. Among the more unusual works are fifteenth- and sixteenth-century examples of a technique associated with Paterna known as *socarrat* (between toasted and burnt). These tiles, designed to be placed between the beams on the ceiling, depict animals, flowers, ships, geometric patterns in spontaneous lines and rough shapes of red or black. The most popular exhibit in the museum is a complete traditional

Colegio del Patriarca

nineteenth-century **Valencian kitchen**, richly decked out in ceramic tiles with panels featuring food and animals.

To see the art of ceramics out in the wild, continue down the street (it becomes Carrer del Poeta Querol after the museum) until you reach the corner formed by the Teatro Principal. Peer up to your left at the upper storeys of the neo-Baroque 1935 triangular building of the **Banco de Valencia**. Above the penultimate balcony is a swath of traditional brightly coloured tilework set against a contrasting red background.

The university and El Patriarca

The streets opposite the ceramics museum lead to two venerable Valencian institutions, the old university and El Patriarca. The Neoclassical university was begun in the fifteenth century, although it is largely the result of later work. It is now a cultural centre, La Nau (open for temporary exhibitions).

Next to the university is the Real Colegio de Corpus Cristi, commonly known as the **Colegio del Patriarca** ⓭ (charge; guided tours by arrangement; booking essential; http://patriarcavalencia.es) in honour of its founder, the sixteenth-century archbishop and viceroy of Valencia, and Patriarch of Antioch, St John de Ribera (1532–1611). Ribera was a leading spirit of the Counter-Reformation, the repressive principles of which he applied in the seminary he founded. The focal point of the complex is a two-storey Renaissance patio composed of a double gallery of arches supported by 56 marble columns shipped in from Genoa. The statue in the middle of the courtyard depicts the archbishop himself, sculpted by local artist Mariano Benlliure.

To one side of the patio is a **church** whose walls and ceilings are entirely covered with richly coloured frescoes by Bartolomé Matarana. Morning mass is in Gregorian chant. Above the altar you'll normally see a beautiful version of the Last Supper by Francisco Ribalta, but during Friday service this is theatrically lowered to reveal a painting of the crucifixion by an anonymous fifteenth-century German artist hidden beneath.

Various works of art are scattered around the Patriarca, including some fine Brussels tapestries. Several rooms are specifically dedicated to displaying an important collection of paintings

NOTES

In the patio of the university stands a statue of Valencian-born Juan Luis Vives (1492–1540), also known as Ludovicus. This brilliant philosopher and humanist spent most of his life outside Spain because of persecution due to his Jewish roots. In England he tutored Princess Mary (later Mary I) and took up a post at Oxford, where he formed close friendships with Thomas More and Erasmus.

Tranquil garden along the riverbed

by Spanish and foreign masters, including El Greco, Juan de Juanes, Caravaggio, Sariñena, Ribalta, Van der Weyden and Morales.

Along the River Turia

Highlights

- **The upper Turia**, see page 54
- **Museo de Bellas Artes**, see page 58
- **Los Viveros and beyond**, see page 58
- **The final stretch**, see page 62

It's not every city that can turn its river into a pedestrian urban freeway, but that is what Valencia has done. After serious floods in 1957, the Turia was diverted through the outskirts to the south, leaving its dry bed still wending through the middle of the city in a large and strategic arc west to east. The bold decision was then taken to transform the former course of the waterway into a ribbon of green for recreational use and the celebration of the arts, and it now serves as an elongated sports and cultural resource, its amenities joined up by walking and bike routes.

For over 6km (4 miles), from the Puente Nou d'Octubre to the Puente de Astilleros, the riverbed is a procession of gardens, sports fields and playgrounds, all planted with a variety of trees, either native to the region or adapted to the climate, notable among them pines, palms, carobs and olives. Between these two crossing points are a further seventeen bridges, seven expressly built as part of the riverbed rehabilitation project. To walk the entire length of the river, begin at Nou d'Octubre station on metro line 3 in the suburb of Mislata (several buses go there too).

The upper Turia

This river of gardens begins upstream in the west with the **Parque de Cabecera** (or **Capçalera**). Next to the public park, the extraordinary **Bioparc** (charge; www.bioparcvalencia.es) is an extensive zoo that recreates different African habitats.

Bioparc is divided into several ecosystems: savannah, equatorial African forest, African wetlands and that of Madagascar. The African savannah includes an acacia forest and is inhabited by zebras, impalas, giraffes and rhinoceros. Lions stretch out on top of large rocky formations overlooking the zebras and antelopes. There is also a palm forest inspired by those found in Kenya, and a cluster of baobabs where a herd of African elephants can be seen drinking at the lake.

Nearby, on Calle Valencia, a continuation of the Passeig de Petchina (which runs along the southern riverbank), is the **Museo de Historia de Valencia** (Valencia History Museum; charge; https://mhv.valencia.es), housed in a nineteenth-century water cistern. The exhibits tell the story of the city from its foundation by the Romans to the present day. Every section is equipped with a 'time machine', consisting of a life-size screen on which actors portray scenes from history in the language of your choice.

Follow the south bank of the river and on the other side of the Puente de Ademuz you'll find the **Museu Valencià d'Historia Natural** ⓮ (Natural History Museum; free; www.mvhn.es). Behind, the **Jardin Botánico** (charge; https://jardibotanic.org) was created on the present site – which was then outside the city walls – in 1802. The university botanic garden is planted with 4500 species organised into twenty collections, including plants useful to humans, a tropical greenhouse, water plants, carnivorous plants, native Valencian species, woodlands and palms. Its most original feature is the Umbraculo, a pergola built of brick and iron.

A little further down the southern riverbank, on the corner of Calle Guillem de Castro, the **Institut Valencià d'Art Modern** ⓯ (IVAM; charge; www.ivam.es) is considered one of the top modern art galleries in Spain. The collection concentrates on Julio González, acclaimed as the father of twentieth-century Spanish sculpture. Its eight galleries include one in which part of the medieval city wall can be seen.

To delve back even further into the depths of history, take a look at the

The elephants are a highlight of the Bioparc

Torres de Serranos

prehistory museum next to the IVAM, the **Museu de Prehistòria de València** ⓰ (charge; http://mupreva.org), in which you can see undeciphered engravings made by prehistoric people living in the hills of Valencia.

Round the bend in the river, just after Puente de San José, is a museum of art of a different kind, the **Casa Museo de José Benlliure** (José Benillure House and Museum; charge). This is the former home of the prominent Valencian painter José Benlliure who died in 1937. There is a pretty garden dotted with authentic Valencian ceramics that you can wander around.

Almost adjacent, the thirteenth-century **Iglesia del Carmen** has a Baroque facade on three levels and an angel as a weathervane. It once formed part of a Carmelite convent but now contains the **Centro del Carmen** (free), a cultural centre and museum displaying Valencian art from the late nineteenth to the early twentieth century.

The next monument you come to, still on the same riverbank, is the **Torres de Serranos** ⑰ (charge). One of the few remaining chunks of Valencia's medieval city walls – and more glamorous than the Torres de Quart – the gateway was built in the fourteenth century using one of the doors of Poblet monastery in Catalonia as a model. It combines defensive and decorative features: its two towers are topped by battlements as if ready for war, but the central panel over the gateway is embellished with delicate Gothic tracery, giving a clue that this is more a triumphal arch than protection. Its structure was left exposed at the back to prevent the towers being used against the citizenry. From the Plaza de los Fueros behind, you can see its various chambers – which have cross-ribbed vaults – once used as a jail for miscreant nobles. Four gargoyles protrude from the rear wall.

Across the next bridge, the Pont de Fusta, is a railway station, once used for a quaint system of narrow-gauge railways but now serving the high-tech tram that departs for the beach. Down this next stretch of the northern bank are two monumental buildings and two gardens. At the end of Puente de la Trinidad, the **Real Monasterio de la Santísima Trinidad** (charge; guided visits only; http://monasteriotrinidad.es) is a working convent inhabited by a closed order of nuns. The monastery door is pure flamboyant Gothic.

NOTES

One part of the Museo de Bellas Artes of particular interest presents the work of three little-known Valencian artists of the nineteenth and twentieth centuries who were inspired by the sea, the colours of the *huerta* and the light cast by the Mediterranean sunshine: Ignacio Pinazo, Antonio Muñoz Degrain and, above all, the Impressionist Joaquín Sorolla.

NOTES

Los Viveros occupies the site of a Moorish country house, later Christian palace and royal residence, which was demolished during the Peninsular War. When the war was over, rubble from the palace was swept together to form two artificial hills, Las Montañitas de Elio, named after the general who ordered their building.

Museo de Bellas Artes

Next to the monastery, the **Museo de Bellas Artes** ⓲ (Museum of Fine Arts; free; www.museobellasartesvalencia.gva.es; free) is housed in a seventeenth-century seminary. This might not compete in size with the large galleries of Madrid and Barcelona but it has an important collection nonetheless, focusing on painting of the Gothic period. You enter via an octagonal vestibule covered by a blue cupola and climb three floors of galleries. The most outstanding pieces are primitive Valencian paintings of the fourteenth and fifteenth centuries, represented by a series of huge golden altarpieces painted in tempera and later, under Flemish influence, in oils by artists such as Jacomart, Miguel Alcanyis, Maestro de Bonastre and Pere Nicolau. Other notable works include Hieronymus Bosch's *Triptych of the Passion*, showing the tormenting of Christ, and Velázquez's self-portrait. There are also works by El Greco, Van Dyck, Goya, Murillo, Ribalta and the local Renaissance painter, Juan de Juanes. It's worth making it up to the top floor where there are works by nineteenth- and twentieth-century Valencian artists.

Los Viveros and beyond

The Museo de Bellas Artes stands at the corner of the city's largest garden, the Jardines del Real, better known locally as **Los Viveros** ⓳ (The Nurseries; free). A wide variety of different spaces are connected by broad *paseos*. There are fountains, pergolas, a restaurant often used for weddings, lawns, ornately decorated benches, bronze and marble sculptures galore and a lake with ducks. Here and there you'll spot intriguing bits of historic architecture salvaged from demolition sites: a Baroque doorway, a pink and grey marble fountain from a monastery, sample houses from the Valencian *huerta*. The garden is the venue of popular concerts in summer and also includes the **Museo de Ciencias Naturales** (Natural Sciences Museum; charge; temporarily closed at the time of writing).

Near Los Viveros, a few steps away from the riverbed, are more gardens, this time protected from the rush and noise of the city by a wall. The **Jardines de Monforte** ⑳ (free) were created in the nineteenth century by Juan Bautista Romero, a wealthy Valencian

Museo de Bellas Artes poster

landowner, and designed by the architect of the bullring. They are Italian in inspiration and Neoclassical in style, with hedges closely trimmed into geometric forms, a long shady arbour, trickling fountains and a scattering of sculptures and marble statues, creating many intimate spaces.

Diagonally across the river from Los Viveros are two churches which would be worth seeing but are hard to visit: the **Iglesia del Temple** (open for mass only; www.iglesiadeltemple.es), which, as its name suggests, owes its origins to the Knights Templar, and the **Iglesia de Santo Domingo** (group visits only by appointment; tel: 96 196 30 03), which has a beautiful Gothic cloister and fifteenth-century chapel but is now owned by the military.

Palau de la Música

Four bridges stand close to each other here, beginning with the stark white **Puente de Calatrava**. Built of extra-tensile steel and with a span of 131m (430ft) supported by a single arch set at seventy degrees from the horizontal, it was designed by the Valencian architect Santiago Calatrava, who is also responsible for the adjacent metro station (and most of the City of Arts and Sciences).

NOTES

The sleek, white Puente de Calatrava has been given the nickname of 'La Peineta' for its resemblance to the ornamental combs worn by women as part of the traditional Valencian costume.

On the city side of the river, the **Plaza Porta del Mar** marks the site of the gate in the city wall that communicated with the harbour. This was the last entry point to be closed at night and anyone absentmindedly arriving late was forced to sleep in the open air across the water, giving rise to the expression 'to be left out under the moon of Valencia', meaning to be left in the lurch. These days the term Luna de Valencia (Moon of Valencia) has been expropriated to refer to the city's nightlife.

A short way further down, the ten-arched **Puente del Mar**, built in 1591, is one of the oldest bridges still standing. Each end is marked by broad flights of steps and the edifice itself is adorned with canopied sculptures of the Virgin Mary and St Paschal.

Continuing down the riverbed parklands, the next sight you come to, beyond the Puente de Aragón, is the **Palau de la Música** ㉑, an ultra-modern concert hall that could almost be a greenhouse for the amount of glass incorporated into its remarkable construction. The main auditorium has such excellent acoustics that the Spanish tenor Plácido Domingo is said to have remarked after his first concert here that 'El Palau is a Stradivarius'. As well as ballet, opera, classical and jazz concerts, the Palau also hosts modern art exhibitions.

Zorbing in front of the Hemisfèric

The final stretch

Over the other side of the next bridge, Puente del Angel Custodio, a giant sculpture of Jonathan Swift's **Gulliver** 22 (free) lies prostrate in the riverbed. With its steps and slides it is a giant, irresistible climbing frame for children.

The last bridge is the longest. The **Puente del Reino** marches 220m (720ft) obliquely across the river, its path lit by Art Deco lampposts. Raised on plinths at either end are the guardians of the bridge: four snarling pseudo-Gothic gargoyles cast in bronze, human of body but with the heads of beasts and half-unfurled wings, they were designed by the engineer who built the bridge, Salvadór Monleón.

There is one more sight of interest on the south bank. The **Museo Fallero** (charge but free on Sun), on the corner of Plaza Monteolivete, honours the tradition of the Fallas, the firework festival held each year in March (see page 91), and houses *ninots*, comic figures in papier-mâché, which have been saved by popular acclaim from the usual conflagration.

The City of Arts and Sciences

Highlights

- **Palau de les Arts,** see page 64
- **L'Hemisfèric,** see page 64
- **Museu de les Ciències Principe Felipe,** see page 64
- **CaixaForum,** see page 65
- **L'Oceanogràfic,** see page 65
- **L'Umbracle,** see page 66

As the former River Turia nears the sea, the new developments along the dry bed reach a climax in the futuristic **Ciutat de les Arts i les Ciències**, the wonderful City of Arts and Sciences. This ambitious cultural complex aims to encourage visitors to combine leisure with an exploration of the arts, sciences and nature. It consists of six ahead-of-the-curve buildings, five of which were designed by Santiago Calatrava.

VISITING THE CITY OF ARTS AND SCIENCES

Except for the Oceanogràfic, it is possible to walk around the City of Arts and Sciences (www.cac.es) at your leisure and enjoy much of the architecture for free. If you want to visit all parts of the cultural complex inside and out, however, you'll need to buy a combined ticket (€40.30) from any of the ticket offices or online, giving admission to L'Hemisfèric, the Museu de Les Ciències Príncipe Felipe and L'Oceanogràfic. This is valid for one, two or three days (they don't have to be consecutive) and permits you to visit each attraction once only.

Palau de les Arts

Approaching from the city, the first of the buildings is a spectacular concert hall, the **Palau de les Arts Reina Sofía ㉓**, which has a 75m (250ft) -high domed roof clad in white mosaic tiles. This was the last part of the complex to be completed. The building houses four separate theatres with a combined capacity of over four thousand seats, designed to provide Valencia with a world-class stage for high-quality opera, concerts, ballet and theatre.

L'Hemisfèric

The concert hall is separated from the other buildings by a bridge, the Puente de Monteolivete, on the other side of which is a hi-tech cinema, **L'Hemisfèric ㉔**, the first part of the city to open in 1998. This eye-shaped cinema has sides like folding portcullises, which open and close in imitation of a blinking eyelid. Its singular aspect has been enhanced by placing it between two symmetrical shallow rectangular ponds. Under what turns out to be an elaborate oval canopy is a sphere stuffed with high technology, where banks of comfortable seats look up at a gigantic, inclined, concave screen 24m (80ft) in diameter. The Hemisfèric's main function is to project the moving images of IMAX films that exceed the limits of human binocular vision, sucking the viewer into the larger-than-life action. It is an overwhelming sensory experience which can be dizzying and disorientating. The cinema is also geared up for laser shows and as a planetarium in which more than nine thousand stars are visible.

Museu de les Ciències Príncipe Felipe

The next building is one of Spain's largest science museums, the **Museu de les Ciències Príncipe Felipe ㉕** (Science Museum; charge), a sloping skeletal structure of steel and glass composed of vast intersecting white arches and taut buttresses. It looks like a cross between a cathedral, a space-age aircraft hangar, and the chalky skeleton of some fossilised sea creature.

The exhibitions are arranged on four floors, though you can wander around some parts of the building, notably Calle Mayor and the terrace, both one level up from the entrance, without paying the admission fee. The contents are fairly standard science museum exhibits, covering life, the Earth, science and technology with many interactive elements.

L'Oceanogràfic, much more than an aquarium

CaixaForum

Duck beneath a road bridge from the science museum and you reach **CaixaForum** (also called L'Àgora; free; https://caixaforum.org/es/valencia), whose spiky ridges look like the blue back of a dinosaur. You can step inside for free to check out the design, but there's a charge for temporary exhibitions and concerts. The interior has some playful features, including hobbit-like buildings and a "cloud" floating in the middle.

L'Oceanogràfic

Further down the riverbed is the final and largest part of the complex, which is technically an aquarium but far more than that. **L'Oceanogràfic** ㉖ (charge; www.oceanografic.org) is made up of a series of lagoons of varying salinity, temperature and depth, designed to represent the five oceans, and pavilions or towers illustrating different marine environments – ocean, wetland, tropical

NOTES

If you are truly in the aquatic mood, you may want to eat in L'Oceanogràfic's underwater restaurant, *Submarino*, where you will be served a seafood meal surrounded by swimming fish. Be warned, though, it quickly gets booked up and you will need to reserve your table as far in advance as you can (www.restaurantesubmarino.es).

sea and the Arctic. The last of these is an appealing igloo-like dome, which is agreeably cool on a hot day outside. The whole place – all three levels of it – is connected by bridges, passageways and underwater glass tunnels – including the longest in the world.

It's certainly an imaginative juxtaposition of architecture and wildlife. There are 10,000 individuals of five hundred different marine species floating above, below or around you or lurking in dark corners of their tanks. Sadly, the aquarium continues to host dolphin shows, which we do not recommend attending.

L'Umbracle

Opposite the science museum and L'Hemisfèric, across another shallow rectangular pond, is **L'Umbracle** (free), a cleverly disguised car park hugging the south side of the complex. The roof has been turned into a winter garden, covered by what looks like a giant white cloche – *umbracle* means arbour or pergola – 18m (60ft) high. It is planted with various shrubs and trees native to Valencia as well as species selected for their adaptation to the climate, and studded with sculptures.

The seafront

Highlights

- **The Port**, see page 69
- **The Paseo de Neptuno and Paseo Maritimo**, see page 69

- **The Cabanyal**, see page 72
- **The Huerta**, see page 74
- **La Albufera**, see page 76
- **Ceramics towns**, see page 78
- **El Puig Monastery**, see page 79

Although much of Valencia's historical prosperity derived from its role as Mediterranean port, until recently the city always kept its distance from – and its back to – the sea. The urban centre grew up just over 5km (3 miles) from the coast, far enough for the harbour area – El Grau – to be thought of as a distinct, unsavoury haunt of rowdy sailors and poor fishermen. In the city centre, meanwhile,

Valencia's sandy beach

there is scarcely a hint of sea nearby except in the name of Avenida del Puerto, built at the start of the twentieth century, leading discreetly off towards maritime perdition.

This relationship only started to shift in the 1960s, when new suburbs filled the void between the two parts of the city. Then came tourism, and hot on its heels, the shabby port was spruced up, a new promenade was built, and controversial plans were mooted (and thankfully unfulfilled) to extend Avenida Blasco Ibañez to the beach by bulldozing part of the historic Cabanyal fishing quarter. The final step in cementing the seafront's reputation as a desirable destination was to host the 2007 America's Cup, whose architectural legacy remains in a scattering of new quayside buildings (see page 11).

The handsome Port Authority building

There are three ways to see the sea. The most direct way is by bus or taxi down Avenida del Puerto, a straight street running from the Plaza Zaragoza. Alternatively, you can take Avenida Blasco Ibañez. By public transport, the most relaxed trip is by tram from the Pont de Fusta station, across the riverbed from the Torres de Serranos; take metro line 4 in the direction of Doctor Lluch and hop off at Les Arenes.

The port

Valencia's port is split neatly in two. The south side concerns itself with the container and passenger terminals (catering for trippers to and from Mallorca and Ibiza), while the northern wharves, adjacent to the beach, have been transformed into a pleasant marina and leisure complex. Some of the more attractive parts of the old port have been preserved on the side nearest the Avenida del Mar, including the handsome **Port Authority Building** with its distinctive clock tower and a handful of warehouses in a restrained mercantile brand of Art Nouveau.

The regeneration centres on a striking modern structure, the **Edificio Veles e Vents** ㉗ (Sails and Winds Building), an iconic water pavilion designed by UK architect David Chipperfield.

Set back from the harbour, next to the church of Santa María del Mar, **Las Atarazanas** ㉘ (Plaza Juan Antonio Benlliure; charge) is an exhibition space housed in a cluster of five Gothic sheds built at the end of the sixteenth century to serve as a workshop for boat building, an arsenal and a place to store maritime tackle. At the time of their building, they stood at the head of the beach.

The Paseo de Neptuno and Paseo Marítimo

Unfurling from the north side of the port is Valencia's flashy esplanade, the **Paseo Marítimo** ㉙. Behind the first stretch is the **Paseo de Neptuno**, a little street lined with restaurants specialising in paella. Each has its back door opening onto the beach and most take advantage of this prime view with glass-enclosed dining rooms and terraces. At weekends and in summer they can be very busy. Prices along the strip vary and some establishments, especially *La Pepica* (https://lapepica.com), trade on long-standing fame.

The Paseo de Neptuno ends at the luxury spa hotel of **Les Arenes**, which retains a pair of restored bright-blue classical temples (entirely rebuilt) that were once part of the old-fashioned restaurant complex that stood here.

From the corner of Las Arenes, the Paseo Marítimo curves along the coastline for 2km (1.25 miles), a palm-shaded multilane pedestrian motorway of dog walkers, pram pushers, joggers and ice-cream-clutching toddlers stretching all the way to the Patacona

Cabanyal architecture

VICENTE BLASCO IBÁÑEZ

Vicente Blasco Ibáñez (1867–1928), Valencia's great son, was a Valencian novelist, journalist and political activist of wide acclaim. Many of Ibáñez's works have been widely translated into English and several turned into films or adapted as TV series. His best-known novels are *Flor de Mayo* (Mayflower), *La Barraca* (The Hut), *Entre Naranjos* (Between Oranges), *Cañas y Barro* (Reeds and Mud) and *Sangre y Arena* (Blood and Sand). With their attention to detail and vivid descriptions, these books create an incomparable record of the traditional fishing and farming methods of Valencia, and the lives of impoverished people in the *huerta* and the Cabanyal quarter, before modern prosperity arrived.

quarter. There is also a cycle track along the length of it. The broad beach of fine golden sand provides a pitch for impromptu games of football or frisbee. The sea, except in exceptionally bad weather, has only a light swell here, and is generally shallow.

One street back from the sea is Calle Eugenia Viñes. Look at the building at No 173 and you will spot two bulls' heads over the door. This is the Casa dels Bous (the House of the Bulls) and is testament to a traditional method of fishing by which heavy boats would be hauled from the surf up the beach by ox teams. The process is famously depicted in paintings by Joaquin Sorolla but you can also see it in a tiled mural, dated 1919, on the top of a house on Calle del Mediterraneo (which runs between the beach and the Cabanyal proper).

For its last stretch, the Paseo Marítimo runs along **Calle Isabel de Villena**, where, in the late nineteenth and early twentieth centuries, wealthy Valencians built themselves fine holiday villas. Among this well-heeled crowd was the novelist and sometime republican-leaning politician Vicente Blasco Ibáñez (1867–1928), who found inspiration in the uninterrupted views of the sea. His reconstructed house is open to the public as the **Casa-Museo**

Blasco Ibáñez (charge; www.casamuseoblascoibanez.es), containing portraits, photographs and sculptures of the writer, as well as books and memorabilia.

The Cabanyal

A few streets back from the Paseo Marítimo is the old fishing quarter of the **Cabanyal** ㉚. This was once a defiantly self-contained community where everyone knew everyone and fishermen would sit on the pavements outside their houses mending their nets. This spirit remains in a few surviving family-run corner shops and neighbourhood bars, the best of which is the *Casa Montaña*, founded in 1836 (see page 117).

The Cabanyal grew up as a patchwork of *barracas* – typical Valencian houses with steeply pitched thatch roofs – aligned in long streets parallel to the beach so that fishing nets could be laid out to dry. Gradually, around the turn of the nineteenth and into the twentieth century, the *barracas* were replaced by small, squat family homes, which were less vulnerable to fire. Many of these were decorated by their owners on the outside in eclectic, highly idiosyncratic styles broadly inspired by Modernismo, the Spanish version of Art Nouveau.

Several of the facades are entirely clad in colourful ceramic tiles, which bounce off heat and humidity and keep the interiors cool. Others, especially near the seafront, are tastefully painted in pastel shades. Everywhere, there are playful details to admire: intricate ironwork ornaments, stucco motifs, a pharaonic head on the tiles of a balcony, a frieze hinting at Moorish Spain, tulips rampant up a door jamb,

NOTES

The Easter week procession through the Cabanyal puts the rest of Valencia to shame with its ostentatious legions of participants dressed as biblical characters, Roman soldiers and, strangely, Napoleonic grenadiers.

Azud de Antella in Jucar River

gargoyles and grotesque heads peering over the street. Look for these fun flourishes on any of the old streets: Reina, Barraca, Padre Luis Navarro, José Benlliure or Escalante.

The entire neighbourhood of Cabanyal is undergoing massive redevelopment with old houses being renovated, pavements widened and streets realigned.

Before leaving, check out the Museu de l'Arròs (Rice Museum; Calle del Rosari 3; charge; www.museodelarrozdevalencia.com), which tells the story of how Valencia's staple foodstuff was produced and processed before industrialisation. Around the city Valencia's hinterland can easily be explored by car, bike or public transport from the city centre. You have a choice of fertile farmland, a watery nature reserve, historic ceramics-making centres or a medieval monastery.

The huerta

While it is possible to visit Valencia without being reminded of the city's proximity to the sea, it isn't easy to ignore the intensely fertile agricultural plain wrapping around the city. Valencians have an almost spiritual attachment to this prime piece of farmland, the *huerta*. From its produce their city originally grew wealthy; later it was relied on to help them survive through hard times; and today the *huerta* continues to fill markets and provide the raw bounty for Valencia's traditional dishes and drinks.

Yet this natural larder is under threat from modernity. Theoretically, the *huerta* covers a semicircle of land roughly bordered by the River Júcar to the south and the hills that start

Oranges are Valencia's major export crop

around Sagunt in the north. In practice, however, it is shrinking rapidly as it is encroached on by the growth of dormitory towns and the inexorable expansion of the outskirts of the metropolis.

But there is still *huerta* remaining and in places you can glimpse how it must have looked in the days when agriculture was a leading industry. At its most perfect, close to the city, the *huerta* is composed of smallholdings where not even the smallest patch of land goes to waste. The fine soil beneath the immaculate rows of artichokes, tomatoes, aubergines and flowers looks as if it has been sifted, fed and spoiled for generations, which it undoubtedly has. Given the warm climate, these plots can produce up to four crops a year when tended with care.

Such high productivity, of course, depends upon water. Crucial to farming the *huerta* are the *acequias* (irrigation channels), whose use and misuse is argued over weekly by the members of the Water Tribunal (see page 39). On its arrival at Valencia, the River Turia is checked by an ingenious system of dams, sluices and overflows, which feeds eight principal *acequias* in proportion to the amount of land they supply. These and other less noble *acequias* crisscross the *huerta*, branching into ever smaller divisions to form a watery labyrinth of glistening channels. The original irrigation system was probably devised by the Romans, but it is the Moors who are credited with perfecting it; they came from Syria, Lebanon and Egypt, where they knew all about the importance of irrigation to farming.

The wealth the *huerta* has generated for some enterprising farmers can be seen in the proud farmhouses – *alquerias* – that poke out from among the foliage. Some have towers and fanciful oriental touches; many are adorned with ceramic ornamentation gleaming in the sun. Much less common are *barracas*: traditional peasant houses with steeply pitched thatched roofs.

One corner of the *huerta*, **Alboraia** ❸❶ has built its fortune on a particular crop, the *chufa*, or tiger nut (*cyperus esculentus*), a brilliant green, spiky plant thought to have been introduced by the Moors. When the tubers are mashed with water and sugar, they become *horchata*, a sweet milky drink served cold in summer (see page 111). The *chufas* of Valencia have their own *denominación de origen*, like wine grapes.

An unusual, scenic way to reach Alboraia is by bike along the Via Xurra Greenway, a cycle track and footpath running from the Torre Miramar roundabout in the city centre. From the seafront, you can cycle to this starting point along the bike lanes either side of the Avenida de los Naranjos, which connects the faculty buildings of the city's university.

Another plant introduced to Spain by the Moors is the humble orange – Valencia's most famous export crop. When the trees flower in late February to early March the sweet smell of the *azahar* blossom perfumes the air. String bags heavy with ripe fruit for sale hang by the side of the road or next to a front door. When buying oranges, don't be put off by their often blotchy or scarred appearance. These "unattractive" fruit, rejected by wholesale export buyers, still have plenty of juice and an intense flavour. The tastiest of the crop, it is said, remains in Valencia.

La Albufera

To the south of the city, where there is even more water available, the *huerta* becomes a checkerboard of paddy fields, sown and flooded in the spring for the rice to mature over the summer. In July and August, the leaves of the crop reach full height, and the landscape flushes a vivid emerald green. Over winter, after the autumn harvest, the terrain turns into a watery maze.

The rice fields converge on **La Albufera** ㉜, a freshwater lake beside the coast that's one of the Iberian Peninsula's prime wetlands for birds. It is easily reached from Valencia by the motorway to El Saler. The lake is fed by the River Turia and flows into the sea through three channels or *golas*, which are fitted with sluice gates to control the water level. It is extremely shallow, up to only 2.5m (8ft) deep, and is gradually shrinking because of natural silting and the reclamation of land by rice farmers. In the Middle Ages the lake was ten times its present size.

If your main interest is primarily wildlife you may want to beeline for **Raco de l'Olla** (by the turn-off to El Palmar), where there is an information centre (free) with a glass-domed observation tower for birdwatching. On the other hand, if you're more interested in food, **El Palmar** is the place to go to eat authentic *paella* and *all i pebre* (eels cooked with garlic and pepper). The village is also the departure point for boat trips around parts of the lake.

If you're feeling adventurous you can try to negotiate the tracks wiggling around the rice fields and along irrigation channels south

Barraca in La Albufera

of El Palmar to the low chapel-crowned hill of **La Muntanyeta de Sants** (the Hill of Saints) and, eventually, the N332 main road.

La Albufera is separated from the sea by a strip of sand dunes and Mediterranean woodland, 10km (6 miles) long and 1km (0.5 mile) wide, called the **Dehesa**, which is fringed with sandy beaches. When the tourists have gone home it is a serene place for an evening stroll.

Ceramics towns

Manises ㉝, next to Valencia's airport, has been synonymous with ceramics since the Moors introduced the craft. The **Museo de Cerámica de Manises** (free; www.museumanises.es) has a

Ploughing the rice fields

BIRDS OF LA ALBUFERA

Well over three hundred species of bird have been recorded in La Albufera, a figure which includes lodgers making a one-off appearance. With patience and binoculars, you are usually sure to spot herons (night, squacco and purple), egrets (cattle and little), ducks, waders, terns and gulls. Shy species like the bittern make good use of the lake's reedbeds and marshy islands, *matas*, to hide in. The bird population spills over into the neighbouring rice fields in search of food.

permanent exhibition of 2500 pieces dating from the fourteenth century to the present day. It's worth taking a stroll around the old town to browse in the ceramics shops and to see some beautiful tiled facades and colourful door jambs.

There is more pottery in **Tavernes Blanques**, a short way north of the city, where the Lladró company has its factory, and the **Centro Cultural y Museo Lladró** (free; www.lladro.com). Visitors see the whole process from design to the kiln, together with an exhibition of current and past products. The Lladró brothers' art collection – including works by El Greco, Sorolla, Zubarán Ribera and other Spanish artists – is on display in a separate hall.

El Puig Monastery

About 15km (9 miles) north of Valencia is the Mercedarian **Real Monasterio del Puig de Santa Maria** 34 (charge; guided tours only; www.monasteriodelpuig.org). In 1237, on the eve of the conquest of Valencia by the forces of King Jaime I, a statue of the Virgin Mary was found on a hill on this spot. A church was built to house the monument, which was adopted as the patroness of the new Christian kingdom. In 1588 the church gave way to the monastery, a forbidding rectangular building with four stout corner towers. The guided visit takes in two cloisters and the refectory, chapel, hall and other rooms where there are numerous works of art.

In one wing, the **Museo de la Imprenta y de la Obra Gráfica** (Museum of Printing and Graphic Arts; charge; www.senadomuseoimprenta.org.es) has a facsimile of what is thought to be the first book printed in Spain: *Les Obres o Trobes en Lahors a la Verge Maria*, printed in Valencia in 1474.

Excursions

Highlights

- **Sagunt**, see page 81
- **Peñíscola**, see page 82
- **Buñol**, see page 83

El Puig Monastery

- **Gandía**, see page 84
- **Xàtiva (Játiva)**, see page 85
- **Denia and Jávea (Xàbia)**, see page 86

Many varied places are within reach of the city of Valencia, especially if you hire a car – although most can be reached with public transport. The easiest to reach are on the coast, or at least on the coastal plain. The nearest are still in Valencia province but rewarding one- or two-day excursions can be made northwards to the Costa del Azahar (the coast of Castellón province) and south towards Alicante and the Costa Blanca. Below are the closest and most worthwhile destinations for a day out.

Sagunt

In 219 BC, Saguntum, a Roman outpost on the Via Augusta whose foundation long predates Valencia, was sacked by the Carthaginian general Hannibal, an attack which was to spark the Second Punic War and lead to the subjugation of Spain by Rome. Among other monuments, the Romans built a **theatre** (free) on the hillside above the present-day town of **Sagunt** 35 (30km/18.5 miles north of Valencia by road or rail), exploiting a natural hollow for its acoustic effects.

In 1896 this theatre was the first building in Spain to be declared a national monument. In the 1980s the decision was taken to rehabilitate it for contemporary performances of drama and music, but the restoration work made controversial use of new materials and techniques and not everyone has been happy with the result.

On the crest of the hill above is a sprawling **castle** (free), which from the fifth century BC was the site of the Iberian settlement of Arse. Over the years it was added to by successive civilisations. Almost 1km (0.5 mile) in length, it is divided into seven plazas or divisions. It frames beautiful views over the town and sea.

Below the theatre and castle, the core of the **old town** is medieval, set around the porticoed main square. The most atmospheric part is the old Jewish quarter, which is laid out in a labyrinth of narrow streets and tiny passageways.

Peñíscola

In the extreme north of Castellón province, the old fortified town of **Peñíscola** (140km/87 miles north of Valencia on the A7 motorway) is built on a rocky promontory into the sea. Its castle, the **Castillo del Papa Luna** (charge), constructed on the foundations of a Moorish fortress, is mainly the work of the Knights Templar and their cross can be seen carved above the door. It later became the residence of the papal pretender Pedro de Luna, cardinal of Aragón, who was elected Pope Benedict XIII during the

Peñiscola, viewed from the Knights Templar castle

Great Schism that split the Christian Church at the end of the fourteenth century. He retired here after he had been deposed and died a nonagenarian in 1423 still proclaiming his right to the papacy. The stronghold was used as a location for the film *El Cid*. Beneath the castle walls, a delightful maze of steep, narrow cobbled streets is lined with white houses, enclosed by massive ramparts and entered by two gates.

To the north of the old town, an immensely long, straight sandy beach stretches to the next resort of Benicarló. There is also a smaller curve of beach to the south, nudging up to the harbour.

Old church in Buñol

Buñol

This small town inland from Valencia is a pleasant enough place but it only tops the tourist wishlist for a single event that takes place on one day of the year: La Tomatina, a massed "battle" using ripe tomatoes as ammunition on the last Wednesday in August. There is nothing strictly traditional about the *fiesta*, which began spontaneously in 1945 as a popular reaction to a parade that went wrong. It has since become internationally famous as "the biggest food fight in the world". Numbers are strictly limited to avoid overwhelming the town, with access by ticket only (https://latomatina.info); be sure to follow the rules laid out for participants.

Inside the Palacio Ducal

Gandía

The Duchy of **Gandía** 36 (65km/40 miles south of Valencia by the A7 motorway) was bought by one Rodrigo Borja in 1485. As Pope Alexander VI he founded the clan known better by the Italian spelling of its name, Borgia. He himself is remembered for his scandalous private life, but his illegitimate son, Cesare, and daughter, Lucrezia, have become definitions of debauchery. The family's reputation was redeemed by Alexander's great-grandson, who was born in Gandía in 1510 and canonised in 1671 as St Francis Borgia. Following the death of his wife, he turned his back on the pleasures of the world, joined the Society of Jesus (the Jesuits) and devoted himself to spreading the ideas of the Counter-Reformation.

For all his saintly work he remained a nobleman and his birthplace, the **Palacio Ducal** (Duke's Palace; charge; www.palauducal.

com), is an opulent building inside, even if no hint of this is given by the simple Gothic courtyard you enter by. The interior decoration, with its painted ceilings and gilded doorways, reaches a zenith in the Baroque Golden Gallery, commissioned by the 10th duke of Gandía to celebrate his ancestor's canonisation. One room on the tour has a concentric circular tiled floor made in Manises representing the four elements of earth, air, fire and water.

Gandía is laced with beautiful sandy beaches and is known for its typical dish, *fideuà*, a kind of *paella* made with *vermicelli* pasta instead of rice (see page 109).

Xàtiva (Játiva)

You can follow the Borgia line backwards by heading inland from Gandía to **Xàtiva** 37 (60km/37 miles southwest of Valencia), the birthplace of the two popes who founded the clan. The Phoenecians are thought to have first settled the site. In the eleventh century, Europe's first paper was made in Xàtiva by the Moors out of rice and straw. A huge ribbon of a **castle** (charge; www.xativaturismo.com/en), with thirty towers, once the most important fortress under the Crown of Aragón, runs along the ridge above the town. On the way up to the stronghold are two very old chapels: the thirteenth-century **San Feliu** (St Felix), which has

THE UPSIDE DOWN KING

Xàtiva was a prosperous place until, as part of the kingdom of Valencia, it backed the losing side in the War of the Spanish Succession, that of Archduke Charles of Austria. Retribution followed the Battle of Almansa in 1707, when the victor, Felipe V, burnt down the town and renamed it San Felipe. In the nineteenth century, the city fathers reclaimed the old Moorish name and exacted their revenge by hanging Felipe's portrait upside down in the municipal museum – and that's the way it has remained.

Jávea cove

a Romanesque doorway, pink marble columns and paintings from the fourteenth and fifteenth centuries, and **San José**, which offers visitors a nice viewpoint outside it.

Among the sights in the narrow streets and small squares of the old town are a former hospital with a Plateresque façade (opposite the sixteenth-century collegiate church), and a medieval fountain in Plaça de la Trinidad. The municipal museum Museo del Almodí (charge), meanwhile, has an unusual royal portrait in its collection worth a gawp.

Denia and Jávea (Xàbia)

The two closest resorts of the Costa Blanca to Valencia are Denia (100km/62 miles south by the A7 motorway) and Jávea (10km/6 miles further), separated by the humpbacked hill and nature reserve of Mount Montgó (753m/2470ft). They are very different in character from each other and between them offer a range of beaches.

The bigger and busier of the two, **Denia** was founded as a Greek colony and named after the goddess Diana. For a while in the Middle Ages, it was the capital of a Moorish kingdom and the oldest parts of its **castle** date from that time. North of the harbour, past the old fishermen's quarter, is the long, wide sandy beach of Las Marinas; to the south is the more discreet and rocky Las Rotas, which has some good snorkelling. In the first two weeks of July Denia holds its Toros a la Mar festival, a bull-run up to the water's edge.

Jávea, over the hill, is in two parts. Its town centre is perched on a hill a short way inland, on the site of an Iberian settlement. Many of the buildings lining the streets – including the town hall and cinema – are made from the local characteristic tosca sandstone. The sixteenth-century church of **San Bartolomé** is an imposing piece of architecture as it was fortified to serve its congregation as a refuge in times of invasion. Over the door are machicolations through which missiles would be dropped on to attackers.

Most buildings around the port and main beach, which are overlooked by a line of ruined seventeenth- and eighteenth-century windmills, are modern but relatively low-level – the legacy of council policy designed to prevent Jávea from being dominated by the high-rise apartment blocks seen in other resorts.

The rest of Jávea's shoreline is rocky. Pirates and smugglers once took advantage of the hiding places afforded by the cliffs, caves and inlets between the lighthouse at Cape San Antonio and Granadella Cove.

NOTES

Many of the older houses in the countryside surrounding Jávea have an unusual feature testifying to the local land use: a *riu-rau*, an arched stone porch where grapes were hung to dry into raisins in the circulating air.

Corpus Christi celebration

Things to do

During the city's frequent *fiestas,* you won't be short of entertainment. There's plenty to do the rest of the year, from browsing local markets to watching opera or attending the theatre. Valencia also has a vibrant bar scene and a handful of outdoor activities, creating the perfect recipe for a city break. To find out what's on during your stay, check out the online listings magazine *Cartelera Turia* (www.carteleraturia.com).

Culture

Music

The principal venues for performances of classical music, opera and ballet are the **Palau de la Música** (Paseo de la Alameda 30, www.palauvalencia.com) and the four performance spaces in the **Palau de les Arts Reina Sofia**, known as **Les Arts** for short (www.lesarts.com; see page 64), which is located in the City of Arts and Sciences.

Rock, pop, jazz and blues are more often to be found in intimate venues such as the **Black Note Club** (Polo and Peyrolón 15; www.blacknoteclub.com).

Theatre and cinema

Most theatrical performances are in Spanish or Valencian, with the occasional appearance from an international company. The main theatre is **Teatro Principal** (Barcas 15; https://ivc.gva.es/val/escena).

Almost all films, whether shown at the cinema or on television, are dubbed into Spanish, but **Filmoteca Generalitat Valenciana** (IVAC, Plaza del Ayuntamiento 17; https://ivc.gva.es) and **Babel** (Calle Vicente Sancho Tello 10; www.cinesalbatrosbabel.com) often show foreign films in their original language with subtitles (look for 'VO' – *version original* – on posters). Most cinemas have three or four showings a day from 4pm to 11pm. Every October Valencia hosts an international film festival, with screenings from the countries around the Mediterranean (https://mostraviva.org).

Nightlife

Valencia is well known for its nightlife – the so-called Luna de Valencia (Moon of Valencia) – nurtured by its benign outdoor climate. Most of the action is in bars called *pubs*, which are a far cry from their British namesakes: in Spain, *pubs* have minimalist decor, loud music and few seats. They open late – the young rarely begin a night out before 11pm – and don't close till the early hours (*pubs* usually after 3am; discos 5am).

Valencia's nightlife shifts location with each new generation. Broadly, it can be divided into four zones. The **Barrio del Carmen** is favoured by bohemians and offers some historical atmosphere to enjoy between drinks. Two well-known bars are **Café Negrito** (on Plaza del Negrito) and **Bolsería** (Calle Moro Zeid 12).

The bars around the Plaza Cánovas del Castillo, on the Gran Via Marqués del Turia, are upmarket and the haunt of the city's rich set. The two other pleasure zones are along Calle Juan Lorens (near the Mercado de Abastos) and the avenidas of Aragón and Blasco Ibañez, and the Plaza de Xúquer, both in the modern parts of town. For an altogether more elegant – and expensive – night out there is the **Juan Carlos I Marina**, at the port end of the beach, with its elegant bars open until late.

The LGBTQ+ scene tends to concentrate in the area around Gran Vía del Marqués del Turia. A popular gay bar is **Turangalila** (Av. Maestro Rodrigo 13; www.turangalila.es), a restaurant with floor shows, while **Mogambo** (Calle de la Sangre 9), beside

NOTES

The prime nightlife time, the small hours of the morning from midnight to daylight, is called *la madrugada*. It comes from the Spanish word, *madrugar*, meaning to get up very early.

the city hall, attracts a mixed crowd. Other busy hangouts include The Muse (Calle de Ruaya 48; www.facebook.com/themusevlc) and Deseo 54 (Calle de Pepita 13–15; www.deseo54.com), a large gay club with drag, dance and DJs plus live performers.

During Las Fallas, a giant flower sculpture of the Virgen de los Desamparados is displayed on Plaza del Virgen

Fiestas

Spanish *fiestas* have to be seen to be believed, and Valencia does them particularly well. Most festivals and events are inspired by an underlying religious pretext of some description, even if at times this is not readily apparent. If you do find yourself in the city during a *fiesta*, forget about doing everything else except enjoying it: streets are likely to be cut off, many shops and museums closed and restaurants and public transport full – but there will not be a dull moment.

Las Fallas

The big event on the cultural calendar in Valencia is Las Fallas, from 12 to 19 March. It's a noisy, riotous, spectacular extravaganza not to be missed. The *fiesta* supposedly originated in medieval times when the city's carpenters would burn their rubbish in the streets outside their workshops on the arrival of spring. Note that hotels are usually fully booked months in advance; plan ahead.

The first week of March, in the lead-up to Las Fallas, sees great processions of people in traditional costume and a *mascletà* – a daylight firework display – in the Plaza del Ayuntamiento every day at 2pm. Then from 12 March until the end, it is commotion all the way. There are concerts in the streets, paella-making competitions, bullfights and people letting off fireworks whenever they feel like it.

On the night of 15–16 March hundreds of *fallas* are put in place throughout the city. Each *falla* – which may be up to 25m (80ft) high – is a set-piece sculpture making a satirical point; figures called *ninots* form mini-scenes within the *falla*. Teams of artists take a whole year to design and build the wood, papier-mâché and fibre-glass figures. To see as many *fallas* as possible, go to a newsstand for a copy of *El Turista Fallero*, which includes a map. The best *fallas* are classed as *sección especial*.

Fallas take up to a year to make

The days of 17 and 18 March are dedicated to the patroness of Valencia, the Virgen de los Desamparados, and a giant floral sculpture of her is made in the Plaza del Virgen. On the night of the 18th there is a firework display in the riverbed. The climax of Las Fallas occurs at midnight on the 19th, when the *fallas* are filled with fireworks and set alight one by one. Last to go up in flames is the biggest *falla* of all, the one in the Plaza del Ayuntamiento, in front of the city hall.

THE FALLAS MAKERS

If Las Fallas seems like a waste of otherwise good pieces of art (and money), consider this: which other city is able to generate an endless supply of work for its artists? A permanent colony of creatives are kept busy in the sixty workshops of the Ciutat Fallera in Benicalap, knowing whatever wonderful creations they dream up and take a year to painstakingly build will be reduced to ashes the following 19 March. Fortunately, a handful of *ninots*, the comic figures that populate the *fallas*, are saved from the flames by a vote each year and placed on display in the Museo Fallero (see page 62).

Easter week (Semana Santa)

The fishing quarter of El Cabanyal stages colourful processions from Palm Sunday to Easter Sunday. Around five thousand people, organised into 27 *cofradias* or brotherhoods, take part. Many dress as biblical characters while others appear as Roman soldiers or, anachronistically, in the uniforms of Napoleonic grenadiers.

The best parades to see are the Silent Procession at midnight on Maundy Thursday and the slow, solemn Procession of the Burial of Christ on Good Friday, which starts around 6pm. The Procession of the Resurrection on Easter Sunday is a more joyful affair, during which the participants throw flowers to the spectators.

Corpus Christi

The Corpus Christi parade (on a date between mid-May and mid-June, depending on the date of Easter) sets off in the late afternoon to the sound of the *tabalet* (drum) and *dolçaina* (a kind of flute) and does a circuit of the streets in the old part of the city around the cathedral. It is essentially an ecclesiastical procession centring upon the great monstrance that is normally kept in the cathedral museum, but the whole occasion is surrounded by colourful traditions. Over 270 people take part as costumed biblical personalities, giants, *cabezudos* (carnival figures with oversized heads), eagle-people and *cirialots* who carry tall candles. In the midst of all of them is La Moma, a person dressed in white with the face covered by a Venetian mask, who symbolises virtue victoriously resisting the seven deadly sins who dance around them. An essential part of the procession are the ten *rocas*, mobile stages on which mystery plays were once performed.

July Fair (Feria de Julio)

This summer celebration has nothing to do with religion and everything to do with livening up the city during a month when citizens are tempted to abandon it for the country or the beach – at least that was the rationale for the nineteenthcentury city council behind the shindig. Most events take place in the Paseo de la Alameda and in the Viveros garden. They include fireworks; rock, pop and jazz concerts; theatre; ballet; and a brass-band competition. There is also a calendar of bullfights in the bullring. The climax, on the last Sunday of the month, is a battle of flowers in the Alameda: an hour of gentle carnation throwing.

Spectator sports and other spectacles

The great spectator sport in Valencia is **football**. The city's internationally successful team, Valencia CF (www.valenciacf.com), plays at the Campo del Mestalla, in Avenida de Suecia, a stadium with a seating capacity of 49,000. Valencia's other team is Levante UD.

Cheste, due west of Valencia on the Madrid road, has a **motorcycle** racing circuit (www.circuitricardotormo.com). **Cycling** competitions take place at the Velódromo Luis Puig (www.fdmvalencia.es/es/instalaciones/palau-velodrom-lluis-puig); **basketball** is played in the Pabellón Fuente de San Luis (www.fdmvalencia.es/instalaciones/pavello-font-de-san-lluis).

Bullfighting takes place at the Plaça de Bous (Plaza de Toros; https://plazadevalencia.es). We don't recommend watching a bullfight, though if you do decide to go, be prepared for what you see: the ritualised killing of animals in an unequal fight. Tickets are expensive and are booked up quickly for important *corridas*. Cheaper seats are in the sun *(sol)*; the more expensive in the shade (*sombra*).

Outdoor activities

The **parklands** of the Turia riverbed are available year-round for anyone who wants to jog, cycle, rollerblade, skateboard, practise athletics or play football. Another good place for a run or bike ride is the Paseo Marítimo beside the beach.

For **swimming** there are Valencia's beaches and an open-air pool in the Parque del Oeste in summer and the indoor swimming pool at the Complejo Patraix (Calle Azagador de las Monjas 10; www.complejopatraix.com) in winter. Other water-sports available include stand-up paddleboarding and windsurfing. The Real Club Náutico de Valencia (Camino del Canal 91; www.rcnv.es) coordinates **yachting** activities.

Tennis players can practise at the University Campus of Universitat de Valencia (Menéndez and Pelayo 19) or take advantage of the courts in the sports complex on Dr Lluch in the Cabanyal.

Valencia has an excellent basketball team

BOAT TRIPS

Boramar (www.boramar.net) and Mundomarino (www.munda marino.es) both run boat trips from a jetty next to Veles e Vents to visit the coast of Valencia. You can choose between a sunset experience, a cruise with a meal or a boat ride with a swim. The maritime scenery is more interesting on a trip from Denia or Javea on the Costa Blanca.

There are six **golf** courses within Valencia province. The closest to the city is Campo de Golf de El Saler (Los Pinares, El Saler; www.parador.es), which has been ranked as one of the best in the world. Other courses near the city are those of El Bosque, Manises and Escorpión.

For information on cycling see page 127.

For other activities, including organised runs and free activities on Cabanyal beach – ask at the tourist information office.

Shopping

Valencia is a pleasant city in which to shop. What it lacks in the specialist or chic retail outlets of Madrid and Barcelona, it makes up for with a good balance between small, old-fashioned family-run stores and ultra-modern shopping centres. Plus, it has the advantage that you can explore most of the shops on foot.

Although manufacturing has declined in favour of service industries, Valencia still offers a few traditional specialities that make good souvenirs: ceramics is its main craft, but locally made leather and wooden goods (guitars, castanets, pipes), fans and, most practical of all, paella pans are all readily available.

Where to look

The modern retail arteries of Valencia lie roughly within an area bounded by the busy streets of Colón, San Vicente Mártir, Játiva and Calle de la Paz. They include Don Juan de Austria, Barcas, Roger de Lauria and Correos. All are within an easy walk of the Plaza del Ayuntamiento. The shopping continues down Jorge Juan and around the Mercado de Colón and along the Gran Vía Marqués del Turia. A handful of traditional craft shops are scattered around the cathedral and behind the Lonja.

Department stores and shopping centres

A good one-stop shop for just about anything is **El Corte Inglés**, a department store (www.elcorteingles.es) with four branches across the city. The main ones are Pintor Sorolla 26 (on the corner of Jardines del Parterre, at the end of Calle de la Paz) for

Pottery stall in Plaza de la Reina

fashion, and Calle Colón 27 for everything else, including books and recorded music.

The closest shopping centres to the city centre, all filled with national and international chain stores, are **Nuevo Centro** (which has a branch of Corte Inglés; www.nuevocentro.es), across the riverbed from the centre, **El Saler** (www.ccsaler.com) and **Aqua** (Calle de Menorca 19; https://aqua-multiespacio.com); the latter two are either side of the City of Arts and Sciences.

Markets and street markets

The **Mercado Central** (Mon–Sat 7.30am–3pm; www.mercadocentralvalencia.es) is a tourist attraction in itself, and the Art Nouveau **Mercado de Colón** (7.30am–2am; www.mercadocolon.es) is also a delight. But for a real feel of the city visit a neighbourhood market such as the **Mercado Ruzafa** (Mon–Sat 7.30am–3pm; http://mercatderussafa.com) or the **Mercado del Cabanyal**

THE LANGUAGE OF THE FAN

Hand-operated air-conditioner, fashion statement, art canvas and even advertising hoarding, the Spanish fan served – and continues to serve – many functions but none more successfully than that of text messenger. In the days when young men and women were forbidden to talk to each other directly without going through a chaperone, a language of fans evolved so that from a distance ladies were able to communicate their desires and arrange trysts from balconies or behind grilles or across ballrooms without anyone else knowing what was being said. There was even an alphabetical fan code which enabled words to be spelled out letter by letter, though due to its complexity it was rarely used. Those in the dating game, however, would be in no doubt as to the meaning of a fan wafted across the heart (I love you), a half-open fan held over the face (they're watching us!) or the use of the fan to shield the face from the sun (you're ugly!).

(Mon–Sat 7am–2.30pm; www.mercadocabanyal.es), near the seafront.

There is a street market every day of the week in one part of the city or another, with stalls selling cut-price clothes and household items. The most important are in **Calle Convento Jerusalén** on Tuesdays, **El Cabanyal** (around the market) on Thursdays and **Benicalap** on Saturdays. Sundays is flea market (*rastro*) day around the **Plaza Redonda**, where an eclectic hoard of vintage and preloved items, including books, plants and art, are ready to be bargained for.

Craft shop on Plaza Redonda

Fashion

The best places to look for designer labels and jewellery are on Colón, Sorní, Cirilo Amorós, Jorge Juan and Ensanche. You'll need deep pockets to shop in this area. **Loewe** has a shop on Plaza de la Reina and Spanish fashion designer **Adolfo Domínguez** has a store at Hernán Cortés 12.

Ceramics and other crafts

The place to shop for ceramics is Manises, but there is a clutch of good shops in the city centre where you'll find a range of household items and ornaments. Try **Artesanía Colla Monlleó** (Plaza Redonda 12; https://collamonlleo.com). Also in Plaza Redonda,

Chez Ramón (https://www.chezramon.es) sells handmade ceramics and wrought-iron lamps. Nearby, at Plaza Milagro de Mocadoret 5, a tiny square through an arch from Plaza de la Reina, **Yuste** stocks ceramics, crafts and custom-made items. **Lladró**, the world-famous porcelain manufacture, has a shop at Poeta Querol 9, facing the ceramics museum.

Traditional Spanish fans – which are perfect for hot, summer days – have been made near Valencia since the fifteenth century. The best place to buy them is **Abanicos Carbonell** (Carrer de Castelló 21; www.abanicoscarbonell.com), a family business that's been going strong since 1810. Ask to see the collection of eighteenth- to twenty-first-century designs. Some are less functional accessories than objets d'art, each one the work of up to twenty different craftspeople.

Paprika for sale at the Mercado Central

Other crafts shops include **Huerta de San Vicente** (San Vicente Mártir 41; https://huertasanvicente.com), which sells craftwork from Andalucía and the rest of Spain; and, for specialist jewellery, **Argimiro Aguilar** (Colón 41; www.argimirojoyero.com).

Fine food and wine

Any large supermarket will stock a range of Valencian and Spanish products. However, the best place to go for fresh produce and spices – and a spot of people-watching – is the **Mercado Central**.

For wines not available in supermarkets, there are several high-class specialist wine shops. These also double as delicatessens, selling fine cheeses, hams, olive oils, *turrón* (a traditional Spanish nougat eaten at Christmas) and other gourmet Spanish products. **Bodega Baltasar Seguí** (Poeta Emilio Baró 17) is family-owned and of long pedigree.

Most *pastelerías* have a good choice for those with sugar cravings. There are sweet shops in Calle Muro de Santa Ana, beside the Torres de Serranos. **Trufas Martinez** (www.trufasmartinez.com) at Calle Ruzafa 12 sells delicious chocolate truffles.

Paella pans

If your culinary experiences in Valencia inspire you to go home and cook your own paella, you'll need the proper pan for the job, and possibly a cooking support for it or gas ring – it is important the heat reaches all the pan evenly. Paella pans come in a range of sizes, from tiny to enormous, and they are classed according to how many people they will serve. The easiest place to find them is outside the **Mercado Central**. You can buy the ingredients inside the market at the same time.

Furniture and antiques

Valencia holds an international furniture trade fair every year and has a wide range of shops in Sedavi, Alfafar, Benetuser and Beniparrell. For classic and avant-garde designs, try **La Oca** at Cirilo Amorós 38 (www.laoca.es).

Calle Músico Peydrò, which runs parallel with San Vicente Mártir, is known for its wicker, cane, bamboo and pine furniture and ornaments. Shops include **Cestería el Globo** at No 16.

Antiques shops and dealers are concentrated in the old town in streets such as Avellanas, Baja and Purisima.

Valencia for children

Children are universally welcomed in Spain at any time of day or night. There are, however, seldom special allowances or facilities for them such as high chairs and kids' portions in restaurants, but waiters and other staff will generally go out of their way to help.

If hiking around the monuments of the city is too much for little legs, a compromise may be to take a ride on the Bus Turistic (www.valenciabusturistic.com), which departs from the Plaza de la Reina. Cycling is a good idea for getting around as a family in an active way. There are also four-seated pedal-powered vehicles available.

Some sights may please both adults and kids. The obvious ones are the **City of Arts and Sciences**, especially **L'Hemisfèric** IMAX cinema and **L'Oceanogràfic**, and the **Bioparc** at the **Parque de Cabecera**. A surprisingly child-friendly museum is the **Museo de Historia de Valencia**, which has life-size display screens. The bed of the River Turia has lots of space to play, and a giant climbing frame in the shape of the Gulliver sculpture is near the Puente del Angel Custodio.

A treat for a day-trip from Valencia is a visit to **Terra Mitica** theme park near Benidorm (www.terramiticapark.com), around an hour and a half each way by motorway.

Festivals and events

5 January Cabalgata de Los Reyes – parade in honour of the Three Kings who arrive on this day bringing children their Christmas presents.

17 January St Antony's Day – pets and other animals are taken to be blessed by a priest on a podium in Calle Sagunto.

22 January Procession in honour of St Vincent the Deacon, co-patron of the city.

12–19 March Las Fallas – festival culminates on 19 March with the ceremonial burning of giant figures.

Semana Santa (Easter week) Processions in the Cabanyal.

Terra Mitica ride

San Vicente Ferrer (Sunday and Monday after Easter) Children act out the miracles of St Vincent Ferrer on a stage set up near his birthplace at the end of Calle de la Mar.

May Fiesta de La Virgen de los Desamparados (second Sunday in May) – festival in honour of Valencia's patroness; a statue of the Virgin is carried in procession from her basilica to the cathedral.

May or June Corpus Christi procession takes place in the streets of the old city around the cathedral.

23–24 June Fiesta de San Juan (St John's Night) – with bonfires on the beach.

July (all month) Feria de Julio – July Fair, ending with the battle of the flowers on the last Sunday.

August (last Wednesday) La Tomatina – a battle with tomatoes in the town of Buñol, west of Valencia; (last Sunday) La Cordá – a spectacular firework festival in Paterna outside Valencia.

September (first week) – grape harvest festival in the wine-growing region of Requeña.

9 October Fiesta de la Comunitat Valenciana – commemoration of the reconquest of Valencia in 1238 by Christian forces with a parade carrying the regional flag leaving from the city hall.

Mid-October Mediterranean Film Festival.

1 November Día de Todos Los Santos (All Saints' Day/Day of the Dead) – people decorate the city's cemeteries with flowers.

Food and drink

Valencian cuisine draws on ultra-fresh fish and seafood from the Mediterranean, prodigious varieties of vegetables from the fertile market gardens of the *huerta*, an abundance of oranges from the surrounding citrus groves and a host of signature rice dishes deriving from the paddy fields south of the city. Whatever you fancy, you will always find something tasty in the city's bars, restaurants and shops. As a bonus, you can eat outside at almost any time of year.

Diverse dining scene

As befits Spain's third-largest city, Valencia's foodie scene is wonderfully varied and suits all budgets. For tapas and cheap eats, head to the area around the Mercado Central, where plenty of places offer set menus for under €15; Barrio del Carmen is also sprinkled with lively tapas bars. The once-gritty Russafa, just south of the centre, has evolved into one of Valencia's coolest neighbourhoods, where you can find everything from Arabic tearooms to vegan and vegetarian restaurants. Valencia has also marched into the gourmet culinary echelons with style and swagger: witness such standouts as *Ricard Camarena* (see page 115). And while the city is the home of paella, the finest places to eat it are, in fact, out of town, in Perellonet or El Palmar, or along the city beach – Paseo de Neptuno is lined with small paella and *marisco* restaurants.

When to eat

Mediterranean Spain's eating hours vary greatly from those of the rest of Europe. For many visitors, the late mealtimes can take some getting used to. Many Spaniards will have only a light meal first thing in the morning – a few biscuits or a piece of toast with a milky coffee, or a glass of fresh orange juice in a bar. They save their appetites for a proper breakfast (*desayuno*) mid-morning, around

10.30 or 11am. It is at this time you will see bars and cafés packed with people tucking into a sandwich or piece of toast for *almuerzo*.

The city's shops and offices close at around 1 or 1.30pm and the bars fill up again, this time for tapas and a beer or wine. First-time visitors are often alarmed at how long Spaniards put off lunch (*la comida*), the main meal of the day – most restaurants won't even open until 1.30pm and will not start filling up until well after 2pm. It is acceptable to sit down for a meal at 3.30pm, a time when the rest of Europe is halfway through the afternoon.

Anyone who has the opportunity will prolong lunch over coffee, and perhaps brandy and a cigar, and then put their feet up for the *sobremesa*, the lazy digestion time after lunch or even have

Plaza de la Virgen in central Valencia

Dishing up paella

a siesta, especially if it is a typically hot Valencia summer day.

At 4 or 5pm the afternoon (*la tarde*) begins. Many people fill the long haul between lunch and dinner with a visit to a café or a *pastelería*, at 6 or 7pm, for something sweet. This stop-gap meal is called *la merienda*.

Restaurants serve dinner/supper (*la cena*) at around 9pm, and many locals may not even sit down to eat until after 10pm. Only those places geared up for tourists will be open before 8pm. However, there are plenty of bars in Valencia where you can eat tapas, and fast-food restaurants open for long hours without a break in the middle of the day.

Where to eat

Every daytime bar or café in Valencia offers at least a few basic tapas and most will make a sandwich or snack to go on command. Many bars morph into no-nonsense restaurants at lunchtime, offering a well-priced set menu for local workers and tourists alike. If you want something fancier, particularly in the evening, you'll need a restaurant dedicated to more formal sit-down meals. The fast-food sector has burgeoned in recent years. Bread shops sell ready-made sandwiches, and there are now several high-quality burger places offering eat-in meals or takeaways.

Top ten things to try

1. Paella

Valencia is the birthplace of paella, Spain's most famous dish. It is a meal to share, at its best when it forms part of a leisurely lunch (never dinner) with friends or family. The genuine version doesn't mix fish and meat – it typically contains chicken, rabbit, *bajoqueta* (green beans), *garrofón* (large butter beans), snails, rosemary and saffron. Two other beans – *ferraura* and *tavella* – are sometimes used as well, and artichokes are added by some chefs. Purists will allow a *paella marinera*, made from seafood instead of meat. It should be prepared fresh and cooked over wood (*leña*), not scooped from some vast, sticky vat; most places will make it for a minimum of two people.

Paella originated as a simple dish that the labourers of the *huerta* could prepare over an open fire during the rice harvest using one shallow, round pan. The first paellas were flavoured with eels – abundant in the wetlands around the Albufera – and eaten communally, straight from the dish, each person with a wooden

FLASH IN THE PAN

Paella is cooked in a particular kind of metal pan (widely available in Valencia in a variety of sizes), by preference over a wood fire but in practice usually over a gas ring. The important thing is for the pan to be level and the heat evenly distributed from centre to rim. Although there are recipes to follow, it takes the skill and intuition of an experienced cook to add the right amount of stock and let it simmer over an even heat, just long enough for the paella to reach the table with the rice cooked to the point of tenderness, neither dry and crunchy, nor moist and mushy. Really good paellas even have a light layer of delicious semi-burnt crust beneath the rice, called *socarrat*, which has to be scraped off the bottom of the pan: paella afficionados consider this a delicacy.

Arroz al horno, a delicious rice-based dish

spoon working his way through an allotted segment, courteously respecting their neighbours' portions.

2. Arroz al horno and other rice dishes

Paella is not the only thing on a Valencian menu – the region excels at rice dishes in general. One of the most popular after paella is *arroz a banda*, rice cooked in fish stock. This was originally a way of using tasty but bone-ridden fish that were trapped in nets and not worth the fuss of eating individually. Restaurants nowadays use good-quality fish, which is served separately to the rice and accompanied by alioli (garlic-flavoured mayonnaise).

Arroz al horno (*arros al forn* in Valencian) has an altogether different taste. This oven-baked dish is made with chickpeas, pork, potato, sausage, tomato, garlic and black pudding. In the days before domestic ovens, housewives would prepare the recipe in an earthenware casserole and take it to the local bakers to have it cooked. Yet another variation on the theme is *arros negre* (black rice), which is made with squid, the ink giving the dish its colour and name.

3. Fideuà

If you want a change from rice, in the La Safor region around Gandía look out for *fideuà*, a kind of seafood paella in which the rice is replaced with vermicelli noodles. The pasta is first lightly toasted, then cooked in a rich seafood broth until it forms a *socarrat*, the coveted crispy bottom layer, just like in paella. The recipe typically includes prawns, squid, tomatoes, onions, *pimentón* (paprika) and saffron, and is served with a dollop of alioli.

4. Tapas

Tapas, little appetising snacks ordered at the bar accompany a glass of wine or beer, are ubiquitous across Spain – indeed, Spaniards will rarely be seen drinking without eating something or other to go with it. Since tapas are available in many places all day long, they are a great way to fill gaps between meals or, if you order enough of them, to replace a meal altogether. There is rarely a tapas menu that can be brought to the table to study. Items may

PAELLA ETIQUETTE

Don't trust any restaurant that offers you an instant paella; the dish needs to be served as soon as it is cooked. You will normally be asked to order at least half an hour in advance, stating how many people it is for (usually a minimum of two). As you finish your appetisers the paella will be brought to your table for your approval and served in front of you. It is best eaten with a squirt of lemon and no accompaniments, except a salad and a pitcher of beer or bottle of wine. Don't be afraid to use your fingers to scoop up prawns, meat and other chunky components.

be chalked up on a blackboard or else staff will reel off a long list of the evening's offerings and, if you're lucky, explain what they are. The simplest way to order is to point to what you fancy – they will be displayed on the counter. If you are stumped, pretty much every tapas bar will do a wedge of *tortilla de patata* (potato omelette), a bowl of marinaded olives, a few slices of cheese (*queso*) and *jamón serrano* (cured ham) or a little dish of meatballs or chorizo, spicy fried potatoes or battered squid.

For something more substantial, you can ask for the same dish as a *ración*, which will be at least double the size of a tapa portion or you can go for an in-between version – *media ración*. Almost anything that comes as a tapa can just as easily be put into a baguette to make a *bocadillo* (sandwich) to eat in or take away.

5. Cakes and pastries

An array of baked goods is to be found in *pastelerías* (cake shops), from *rollitos de anis* (aniseed-flavoured biscuits) and *rosegones* (small, hard almond biscuits) to *pasteles de boniato* (pies of sweet yam) and *susus*, sticky doughnuts filled with a creamy custard. At Easter, soft and subtly sweet *panquemado*, literally 'burnt bread' but in reality something akin to brioche, makes a good breakfast or pairs well with an afternoon coffee. As for sweets, Valencians are expert in turning almonds into all things delicious. *Turrón* (nougat) and *mazapanes* (marzipan), favourite Christmas treats, are made in Alicante, inland from the Costa Blanca. The town of Casinos, in the hills northwest of Valencia, is known for its *peladillas* – whole almonds covered in sugar.

6. Horchata

Horchata, a sweet milky drink made from crushed tubers (tiger nuts), originates from Alboraia, just outside Valencia. In the city centre, head to *Santa Catalina*, a *horchatería* off Plaza de la Reina, but for an iconic experience, you need to beeline for Alboraia

Horchata is made from crushed tiger nuts

itself, specifically *Horchatería Daniel* (www.horchateria-daniel.es). Popular all over Spain, this refreshing summer drink is always served cold and is available as a liquid (*liquida*) or semi-frozen (*granizada*). If you're feeling peckish, copy the locals and dip soft sweet cake sticks (*fartons*) or crunchy breadsticks (*rosquilletas*) into it. Although you can now buy packaged *horchata* all year-round in supermarkets, it is not comparable to the fresh product. *Horchata*-making often goes with ice cream and Valencia has a reputation throughout Spain for producing the best in the country – a skill supposedly derived from its historical connections with Italy.

7. Chocolate con churros

A Spanish favourite, eaten mostly in winter, is *chocolate con churros*: sugar-dusted, deep-fried batter sticks (*churros*) dunked into thick, hot drinking chocolate (or coffee if you prefer). These are traditionally eaten at breakfast time, though you can usually pick them up throughout the day.

8. Agua de Valencia

If you bar-hop your way around the city, you'll almost certainly come across Agua de Valencia, a cocktail of sparkling wine, orange juice and vodka. This smooth concoction slips down all too easily – you have been warned.

9. Utiel-Requeña wines

While Valencian vineyards are generally not well known outside the region, they are gradually making a reputation for themselves. Those of Utiel and Requeña, the main growing areas, produce some good rosés and medium-strength dry reds. If you prefer dry white wines, these are produced in the cold continental climate of the Alto Turia district.

Calamares a la romana

10. Leche merengada

Another popular drink served by cafés and *horchaterías* across Valencia is *leche merengada*, a kind of milkshake with egg and sugar added and flavoured with lemon and cinnamon, served cold and sweet.

To help you order

I'd like to reserve a table for two/four people. **Quiero reservar una mesa para dos/cuatro personas.**

Could we have a table for two/four people? **¿Tiene una mesa para dos/cuatro personas, por favor?**

Do you have a set menu? **¿Tiene un menú del día?**

I'd like a/an/some… **Quisiera...**

The bill please **La cuenta, por favor**

Thank you **Gracias**

Menu reader

aceite oil
agua water
al ajillo in garlic
a la plancha grilled
a punto medium
arroz rice
asado roasted
atún tuna
azúcar sugar
bacalao salt cod
bocadillo sandwich
boquerones anchovies
bien hecho well done
calamares squid
cangrejo crab
caracoles snails
cerdo pork
cerveza beer
champiñones mushrooms
chorizo spicy sausage
cocido stew
cordero lamb
ensalada salad
entremeses hors-d'oeuvre
gambas prawns
helado ice cream
jamón serrano cured ham
judías beans
langosta lobster
leche milk
mariscos shellfish
mejillones mussels
pan bread
patatas potatoes
pescado fish
picante spicy
poco hecho rare
pollo chicken
postre dessert
pulpitos baby octopus
queso cheese
tortilla omelette
verduras vegetables
vino wine

Places to eat

Each restaurant and café reviewed in this Guide is accompanied by a price category, based on the cost of a three-course meal (or similar) for one, including wine, cover and service. For tapas, these prices can only be approximative because it depends on what you order – and how many plates.

€€€€ = over €60
€€€ = €30–60
€€ = €20–30
€ = below €20

City centre

Restaurants

Atenea Sky Moratin 12, www.ateneasky.com. A rooftop restaurant on the eighth floor with a spectacular view over Valencia's central square. There is a choice of outdoor or indoor tables. There is another restaurant with an almost identical name, the *Ateneo*, on the sixth floor of the same building, which is slightly cheaper but just as good – only without the fine view. Daily noon–1.30am. **€€**

La Cigrona Serranos 22, www.lacigrona.com. Mediterranean cuisine not far from Torres de Serrans. Mains might include Spanish garlic shrimp, delicious patatas bravas, beef-tenderloin tacos with spring garlic and baked potatoes or cuttlefish with honey, prawns and artichokes with Sichuan pepper; finish with profiteroles with chocolate sauce and almond *crocanti*. Wed–Sat 1.30–4pm, Sun 1.30–4pm. **€€**

Clann Assaonadors 9, www.clannvalencia.com. A glorified tapas bar in the heart of the Barrio del Carmen, which is thoroughly Valencia but, as its name suggests, with Irish influences. Surprisingly, though, is said to serve the best tapas in town – judge for yourself – but *Clann* also does full meals. **€€**

Ricard Camarena Avenida de Burjassot 54, Bombas Gens Centre d'Art, www.ricardcamarenarestaurant.com. This Michelin-starred restaurant owned by renowned chef Ricard Camarena has a modern, minimalistic, albeit cosy, wooden interior. It offers a fusion of typical Valencian flavours and ahead-of-the-curve culinary art. A short daily menu includes plenty of fresh regional Mediterranean ingredients, including seafood, vegetables and rice, all prepared in the most creative way. Book well in advance. Closed Mon. The same chef has a less formal bar in the Mercado Central. **€€€€**

La Riuà Calle de la Mar 27, www.lariua.com. *La Riuà* has been serving home cooking by a family team since 1982. Its Valencian cuisine includes a wide range of rice, fish and shellfish dishes, and the legendary kitchen is acclaimed for its paella, *fideuà* and *all i pebre* (eel stew). Book in advance. Closed Sun night and Mon. **€€**

Taberna Alkazar Mosén Femades 9 and 11 (Zona Peatonal), www.tabernaalkazar.com. The *Alkazar* is an upmarket seafood and paella restaurant that first opened its doors in 1950. Choose a table inside or outdoors in the pedestrianised street. There's a busy tapas bar if you don't feel like a full meal. Large selection of wines. Mon–Fri 11am–midnight, from 11.30am Sat & Sun. **€€€**

Tapas bars

100 Montaditos Plaza de la Reina 10, http://spain.100montaditos.com. One of a chain of bars in a traditional style that specialise in inexpensive tapas, especially, as the name says, one hundred different kinds of open sandwiches or *montaditos*. They also serve sharing plates, alongside pizzas and salads. **€**

La Pilareta Moro Zeit 13. *La Pilareta* is one of the oldest tapas bars in the city, dating from 1917, and remains as famous as ever for its exceptional mussels. **€**

Along the river

A Tu Gusto Escritor Rafael Ferreras (on the corner with Avenida Instituto Obrero), www.atugusto.com. Relaxed place a few streets away from the City of Arts and Sciences, where you can enjoy creative Mediterranean dishes and a very good-value lunchtime menu. Closed Mon. **€€**

The Fitzgerald Burger Company Ribera 16, www.thefitzgerald.es. Conveniently close to Plaça de l'Ajuntament, this fast-food haunt dishes up the best burgers in town. Other specialities include delicious chicken nuggets, chicken wings and crunchy fries. There are four more branches in the city. Sun–Thurs 12.30–11.30pm, Fri & Sat until midnight. **€€**

Marisquerías Civera Mosén Femades 10, www.marisqueriascivera.com. Fish and seafood restaurant of long standing in the historic city centre. There are also some meat and vegetarian options. Open daily for lunch & dinner. **€€€**

City of Arts and Sciences

Novaterra CaixaForum, https://caixaforum.buenacarta.com/en. The restaurant in the CaixaForum arts centre does a reasonably priced lunchtime menu. Vegetarians and vegans are catered for, plus there are children's dishes available. **€**

Submarino L'Oceanogràfic, www.oceanografic.org/restaurante-submarino. This atmospheric and romantic underwater dining space allows you to watch sealife glide by the glass at L'Oceanogràfic aquarium. Reservations are essential. **€€€**

The seafront

Restaurants

Destí 56 Paseo de Neptuno 56, https://destino56.es. Gaze out to sea at this beachfront haunt on Playa de las Arenas. Expect modern décor, sizzling paella and fancy cocktails. Mon–Thurs 10am–2am, Fri until 3am, Sat & Sun 9am–3am. **€€**

La Pepica Paseo de Neptuno 6, www.lapepica.com. A classic Valencian restaurant founded in 1898 and visited by Ernest Hemingway and other writers, as well as bullfighters, artists and assorted VIPs. It is set on a beachfront street packed with paella restaurants – some cheaper and where, arguably, you can eat just as well. *La Pepica* is a cut above the rest, though, not only for its rice dishes but also its lobster stew and grilled fish. Try the house speciality paella. Daily lunch, Fri & Sat also dinner. **€€€**

La Sucursal Muelle de la Aduana, https://veleseventsvalencia.es. With a Michelin star under its belt, *La Sucursal* offers not only the very best of Valencian haut cuisine but also splendid views over the boat-speckled marina. Mon–Fri lunch & dinner, Sat & Sun dinner only. **€€€€**

Taj Mahal Doctor Candela 20, www.restauranteindiotajmahal.es. Excellent Indian/Pakistani restaurant, decorated with handicrafts and paintings, in the suburbs between the city and the seafront. All the spices are imported from the Indian subcontinent. Good vegetarian options. Open daily for lunch & dinner. **€€**

Tapas bars

Casa Montaña José Benlliure 69, www.emilianobodega.com. This tapas bar, which was founded in 1836, has been transformed into a tasting centre for fine wines. Around a thousand types from around the world, but especially Valencia, can be ordered by the glass. All the dishes on the menu are made from carefully selected ingredients and include mussels, grilled sardines, squid, anchovies, typical Cabañal recipes, codfish croquettes and different Spanish cheeses and cold meats. Open daily, only lunch on Sun & holidays. **€€**

Outskirts

Blayet Avenida Gaviotas 17, El Perellonet, http://blayet.com. This inviting spot south of the Albufera, part of a hotel with sea views, has been ladling out fragrant paellas and fresh seafood since 1935. Book ahead on weekends. Closed Feb. **€€€**

La Matandeta Carretera Alfafar–El Saler km 4, Alfafar (7km/4.5 miles from Valencia), www.facebook.com/lamatandeta. Fresh fish and seafood served in a typical country house in the *huerta*. Here, paella is cooked over an open wood fire, which gives the dish a delicious smoky flavour. Tues–Fri 10.30am–5pm, Sat & Sun 10am-6pm. **€€€**

Raco' Nou Carretera de El Palmar 21, El Palmar, www.nouraco.com. Feast on classic Valencian cuisine at this long-established restaurant, including a variety of rice dishes, seafood and *all i pebre* (eel and potato stew) – all pleasantly served up beside La Albufera. Set-menu options available. **€€€**

El Rek Pintor Martí Girbés 1, El Palmar, www.arroceriaelrek.com. *El Rek* is located outside the town of El Palmar, in the heart of Valencia's rice-growing area and beside La Albufera. The menu consists of traditional Valencian cuisine, including paella, *arroz a banda* (rice cooked in fish stock) and *arroz negro (with squid ink)*. The restaurant has its own jetty from which you can take boat trips around the lake. Wed–Sun 1–5pm. **€€**

Restaurante Robert Anguilera, 7, El Saler, www.hostalandres-elsaler.es. A great spot in the heart of La Albufera serving up a bit of everything –

cooked well and for all times of the day. The menu is adorned with tapas and typical rice dishes of the region, such as *caldosos* (in broth), alongside fresh fish, grilled meats, pizza and pasta. Breakfast and food to take away are also available, perfect for picnics on the beach. Suitably tempting desserts include cheesecake and tarte tatin. Rooms available too. **€€**

Buñol

Venta Pilar Avenida Pérez Galdós 5, www.posadaventapilar.com. At around 300 years old, this former staging post turned hotel restaurant serves simple, home-made food. The daily menu offers excellent value compared with the more expensive à la carte options. Dishes, which include local as well as Spanish specialities, can be served in one of the dining rooms or on the outdoor patio. Try one of its wonderful, smoky rice plates prepared over an open fire. There's also a 1960s-style café which does breakfast and lunch. **€€**

Cullera

Casa Salvador L'Estany de Cullera, www.casasalvador.com. *Casa Salvador* is set in a pair of *barracas* (typical Valencian farmhouses) next to a freshwater lake used for fish farming. The family business claims to have been open every day for the last fifty years. Choose from a wide range of rice, fish and other typical Valencian dishes, including *arroz negro* (squid ink rice) and whole fish baked in a salt crust. The outdoor terrace overlooks the lake. Open daily 10am–5pm & 8pm–midnight. **€€€**

Denia

Quique Dacosta Restaurante Urbanización El Poblet, Carretera Les Marines 3km, http://quiquedacosta.es. This three-Michelin-starred restaurant is famous for its innovative twist on Mediterranean cuisine. The 'DNA the Search' menu pays homage to regional culinary traditions while being blended with the chef's boundless imagination and creativity. Booking is essential. Wed–Sun lunch & dinner. **€€€**

Gandia

Telero Sant Ponc, 7 Bajo, www.telero.es. Friendly atmosphere and excellent service make this homely restaurant the perfect place to try traditional Valencian cuisine. The rice dishes and tuna steak are highly commendable. Vegetarian and gluten-free dishes also available. Good choice of regional wines. Closed Sun. **€€**

Peñíscola

Casa Jaime Avenida Papa Luna 5, https://casajaimepeñiscola.com. The menu is dominated by rice dishes and fresh fish from the coast of Castellón. Fine selection of home-made desserts. Closed Wed in winter. **€€€**

Sagunt

Arrels Castillo 18, www.restaurantarrels.com. Dine beneath Gothic, Romanesque and Mozarabic arches in this garlanded restaurant set in a restored sixteenth-century ducal palace on the road towards the castle. Closed Mon, dinner only Thurs, Fri & Sat. **€€€€**

Xàtiva

Casa La Abuela Calle Reina 17, tel: 96 227 05 25. 'Grandmother's House' has changed over its fifty-year existence from a simple restaurant into a renowned establishment, though it remains true to traditional local recipes, particularly Valencian rice dishes. The excellent *arroz al horno* (oven-baked rice) is worth a try. Closed Wed. **€€€**

Travel essentials

Practical information

Accessible travel

Museums, hotels and restaurants in Valencia are almost all equipped for people with reduced mobility. Still, you will still be wise to research facilities before you start your trip. A very helpful place to begin is www.visitvalencia.com/en/valencia-accesible, which offers a guide to accessible accommodation, restaurants, leisure facilities and transport. The city has created a series of sixty pictograms to help those with cognitive challenges find their way around more easily.

Accommodation

Spanish hotels are awarded one to five stars according to their facilities – a system that tells you nothing about quality, views or the history of the building, let alone intrinsic personality. Hostels (*hostales*, denoted by the letter H outside) and *pensiones* (boarding houses, denoted by the letter P) are more modest places to stay with fewer facilities. Both are graded with one to three stars. The official tourist information website, www.visitvalencia.com, includes hotel listings.

Valencia's best hotels get booked up quickly for trade fairs and the Fallas festival in March. In general, prices are quoted per room and breakfast is rarely included. Value-added tax (IVA) may or may not be included in the quoted price so it is best to confirm this.

A wide range of self-catering accommodation is also available, booked through agency websites and only occasionally directly with the owner.

When deciding where to stay, you will need to choose between three main areas: the city centre, the beach, and the modern suburbs around the City of Arts and Sciences. Consider where you want to spend most of your time to reduce your dependency on transport.

I'd like a double/single room. **Quisiera una habitación doble/individual.**

with/without bath/shower double bed **con/sin baño/ducha cama de matrimonio**

What's the rate per night? **¿Cuál es el precio por noche?**
Is breakfast included? **¿Está incluído el desayuno?**

Airports

Valencia's international airport (www.aena.es/en/valencia.html) is at Manises, 8.5km (5 miles) from the city. You can reach the centre by bus #150 (€1.45 full fare; the journey takes about 40min, depending on traffic) or metro lines 3 or 5 (approximately the same journey time as the bus). Metro line 5 runs all the way to the port and seafront. The airport is in zone B: if you are using a travel card, make sure you have sufficient credit for the route (see page 139). Taxis line up outside the arrivals hall.

Apps

The official Visit Valencia app can be useful for finding information on sights and tourist routes. It's especially good for discovering what's on and booking tickets for events.

Beaches

Valencia's warm climate means the many long, sandy beaches accessible from the city can be enjoyed for several months of the year. They get busy during the holiday period of July and August (especially the latter), and at weekends in June and early September.

The **Playa de Las Arenas** and **Playa de la Malvarrosa** together comprise the city's main beach, which is easy to reach from the centre by buses #95, #99, #32, #31, #1 and #19. The best mode of transport is the tram (metro line 4): hop on at Pont de Fusta station, which is over the riverbed from the centre. Metro lines 5 and 7, from Xàtiva and Colón in the centre, also run close to the seafront but you will have to walk the last bit of the route or take a connecting tram from Marítim station.

The two most popular beaches to the north of Valencia are **La Pobla de Farnals** and **Port Saplaya**, both within easy reach by car (the former also by metro line 3). To the south the principal beaches are **Playa de Pinedo**

(6km/4 miles from Valencia) and **Playa del Saler** (12km/7.5 miles), which are accessible by taking the motorway to the town of El Saler and then the coast road, CV-500. There is also a bus service there (#24 and #25).

Budgeting for your trip

Transport to Valencia. For Europeans, Valencia is a short and affordable direct scheduled flight away from many major cities. However, if you are travelling from beyond Europe the flight will be a considerably greater proportion of your overall budget.

Accommodation. Hotels in Valencia are quite expensive, especially in the height of summer, but many offer special off-peak deals. Self-catering can be an economical option, especially off-season. A cheaper, though less convenient, option is to stay outside Valencia – although, of course, your transport costs will increase. Wherever you stay, it is always wise to book ahead for the best deals.

Meals. Eating out is not always cheap, though with favourable exchange rates, even top-rated restaurants may be surprisingly affordable compared to many European capitals. The *menú del día*, a fixed-price midday meal, is an excellent bargain available in most places, even fancy ones. Spanish wines are reasonably priced.

Local transport. The sights in the city centre are mostly within walking distance of each other, making public transport use often unnecessary. However, if you do venture further afield, public transport in Valencia is inexpensive and even taxis are affordable.

Museums and monuments. Some, but not all, of Valencia's museums and galleries charge for admission. Note that many institutions are free on Sundays and closed on Mondays. Most places offer reduced admission for children and the elderly.

Valencia Tourist Card. This card permits the holder to travel free on public transport (including the airport route) and offers discounted entry to museums and other tourist sights, entertainment venues, shops and restaurants. It is available in one-, two- or three-day forms for €15, €20 and €25, respectively (there is also a seven-day card without transport for €12).

The discounts aren't always huge and it's worth considering exactly which monuments you plan to visit and how much you will use public transport before you invest in a card. It is available from tourist information offices, bus stations, hotels, tobacconists and online (with a ten percent discount). For more details visit www.visitvalencia.com.

Camping

Valencia's climate makes camping quite easy for most of the year. There are three campsites to the south of the city, close to the sea and the Albufera nature reserve: **Camping Coll-Vert**, Playa de Pinedo, Carretera del Riu 486, www.collvertcamping.com; **Camping Devesa Gardens**, Carretera del Saler, km 13, www.samay.com; and **Camping Puzol**, Camí riu Turia 3, Playa de Puzol, www.campingpuzol.com.

Car hire

You won't need a car to explore the city because the public transport system is so good. Besides, the traffic can be disconcerting and finding a parking space is often tricky. However, if you decide to make trips beyond the urban area you'll find having your own transport will give you more flexibility.

The main car-hire companies have offices at the airport and in the city. Among them are **Enterprise Rent a Car** (www.enterprise.com), **Avis** (www.avis.es); **Hertz** (www.hertz.es); and **Europcar** (www.europcar.es).

To hire a car, you must be over 21 and have had your driving licence for at least a year – citizens of the EU can use their normal licences; other nationals need an international one.

Before setting off, read the Driving section below.

I'd like to hire a car tomorrow/for one day/a week. **Quisiera alquilar un coche para mañana/por un día/una semana.**

Please include full insurance. **Por favor incluya el seguro a todo riesgo.**

Climate

Valencia is graced with sunshine for most of the year, and has an average annual temperature of 17°C (63°F). The best seasons to visit are spring and autumn, although sometimes there is light rainfall in both. Summers can be hot and humid, but winters are mild, with a temperature that rarely falls below 10°C (50°F). However, climate change has destabilised the pattern and you are advised to check before you travel so you are prepared for any freak weather conditions. The average monthly highs and lows are given below:

	J	F	M	A	M	J	J	A	S	O	N	D
°C	13	14	16	18	21	25	28	28	25	21	16	13
	6	7	9	11	14	18	21	21	19	15	11	8
°F	55	57	60	65	71	78	82	82	77	69	62	56
	43	45	48	52	57	65	69	69	66	58	51	46

Crime and safety

Valencia is one of the safest cities in Spain, but common sense and caution should prevail at all times, especially in crowded metros, squares or bars. It is advisable to avoid small, unlit streets and parks after dark.

Otherwise, precautions include: never leave bags unattended; don't carry too much money with you; attach your phone to your body if you can; and photocopy your personal documents and leave the originals in your hotel's safe, along with your valuables. Don't leave anything on display inside your car.

If you are the victim of a robbery, visit the nearest police station (*comisaría*) and make a report (*denuncia*); you will need it for your insurance claim. For the local police, call 092.

I want to report a theft. **Quiero denunciar un robo.**
My ticket/wallet/passport/telephone has been stolen. **Me han robado mi billete/cartera/pasaporte/teléfono.**

Cycling

Valencia is the ideal city for exploring by bike. The climate is warm for most of the year and there are no hills, which means that the only slopes you will have to negotiate are in and out of the riverbed. Beyond the city centre, an excellent network of paved and clearly marked cycle lanes follows the main thoroughfares, with dedicated traffic lights for cyclists at intersections. In the narrow winding streets of the city centre, you might prefer to walk, but if you do decide to cycle, choose the streets marked "Ciclocalle" – but expect to share them with pedestrians and a limited amount of motor traffic.

Note that cycle lanes are also used by e-bikers, scooter riders and roller-bladers. Not all of these other road users are considerate and law-abiding, so always check what is coming up behind you before making any sudden manoeuvres.

The most popular cycle route in Valencia is along the riverbed, which is entirely traffic-free. Many people also pedal out to the seaside to the bike lane that follows the Paseo Marítimo at the head of the beach (see page 69). For more of a challenge you might want to take a lesser-touristed route. Before setting off, familiarise yourself with the geography because occasionally the bike signposting can be confusing, and you can't always rely on online maps and navigational tools in remote areas. Cycling to the Albufera, its beaches and the paddy fields is a good way to spend a day but it's around 20km each way, depending on exactly where you go. Another worthwhile excursion takes you 15km into the *huerta* on the Via Xurra Greenway; the route starts near the large Torre Miramar roundabout in the north of the city.

For more ideas, visit www.metrovalencia.es/en/the-metro-is-yours/bicimetro, which outlines 24 'Bicimetro' cycle routes, including distance and difficulty rating, which are just an easy metro journey away. Note: e-bikes aren't allowed on the metro.

The city's public bike network is Valenbisi (www.valenbisi.es), which offers a simple and efficient way to get around 24/7. You can pick up (and later leave) a bike at any one of 276 stations across the streets. The first 30min is free.

When cycling, it is advisable to wear a helmet and to carry water, a bike lock and a pump.

Many companies rent out bicycles, e-bikes, pedal-powered cars and powered scooters. Some companies also run group guided tours, including:
Cyclobikes Valencia Turia gardens, next to Gulliver Park, www.cyclobikes valencia.com.
Do You Bike Calle del Mar 14 (and two other locations), www.doyou bikerental.com.

Driving

When driving in Spain you must be over 18 and carry with you the following documents: your passport, a valid driving licence, registration papers and a Green Card (international insurance certificate for non-EU countries) or a national insurance certificate (EU member states).
Road conditions. Outside of the morning and evening rush hours, Valencia's roads aren't too congested for a big city. However, expect traffic jams on entry roads into the city on Sunday evenings and after holiday weekends.
Motorways. Valencia city and province are well served by main roads and motorways. The A7 running north–south between Catalonia and Alicante and the motorway heading west towards Madrid are toll-free.
Rules and regulations. You should display a nationality sticker on your car. Most fines for traffic offences are payable on the spot, although a speeding fine may be sent to your home address even if it is outside Spain. Drive on the right and overtake (pass) on the left. Give right of way to vehicles from the right (unless your road is marked as having priority). The use of seat belts is compulsory.

Speed limits in Spain for cars are 120km/h (75mph) on motorways, 100km/h (62mph) on broad main roads (two lanes each way), 90km/h (56mph) on other main roads, and 50km/h (31mph) – or as marked – in densely populated areas.

Spanish law requires that you should carry a reflective safety jacket and a warning triangle in your car for use in the event of a roadside emergency.

driving licence **carnet de conducir**
car registration papers **permiso de circulación**
Can I park here? **¿Se puede aparcar aquí?**
Are we on the right road for…? **¿Es ésta la carretera hacia…?**
Where does this road lead? **¿Adónde va esta carretera?**
Fill the tank please **Llénelo, por favor**
top grade **con super**
petrol **gasolina**
unleaded petrol **gasolina sin plomo**
diesel **gasoléo**
Please check the oil/tyres/battery. **Por favor, controle el aceite/los neumáticos/la batería.**
I've broken down. **Mi coche se ha estropeado.**
There's been an accident. **Ha habido un accidente.**

Road signs. Some of the street names and signs are in Valencian. Most essential road signs, however, use the standard European pictographs. The translations below could be useful:

¡alto! stop!
aparcamiento parking
autopista (de peaje/peatge) (toll) motorway (expressway)
ceda el paso give way (yield)
curva peligrosa dangerous bend
despacio slow
desviación diversion (detour)
entrada entry
estacionamiento prohibido no parking
obras roadworks
¡pare! stop!

peatones pedestrians
peligro danger
salida exit (from motorway)

Electricity

The standard is 220-volt. Sockets take round, two-pin plugs. Visitors from North America will need a transformer unless they have dual-voltage travel appliances. Transformers and adapters can be bought in most hardware shops.

Embassies and consulates

All embassies are in the national capital, Madrid.
Australia www.spain.embassy.gov.au
Canada www.international.gc.ca/country-pays/spain-espagne/madrid.aspx
Ireland www.ireland.ie/en/spain/madrid
New Zealand www.mfat.govt.nz
South Africa www.dirco.gov.za/madrid/en
UK www.gov.uk/world/organisations/british-embassy-madrid
US https://es.usembassy.gov

Emergencies

For a general emergency *(emergencias)*, call **112**. Otherwise, telephone:
Ambulance: **061**
National Police *(policía nacional)*, in and outside Valencia: **091**
Local police *(policía local)*: **092**
Fire *(bomberos)*: **080**
Guardia civíl (outside the city): **062**

Fire! **¡Fuego!**
Help! **¡Socorro!**
Stop! **¡Deténgase!**

Call the police/an ambulance **Llame a la policía/a una ambulancia**
Where is the nearest hospital? **¿Dónde está el hospital más próximo?**

Getting there

By air. Valencia's airport (see page 123) receives direct scheduled flights from airports across Spain and Europe and from Morocco and Algeria. Services from the rest of the world connect via Madrid and Barcelona. Spain's national carrier is Iberia (www.iberia.es). The low-cost airlines offering flights between Valencia and the UK are Ryanair (www.ryanair.com), easyJet (www.easyjet.com) and Vueling (www.vueling.com).

By sea. Valencia's port (www.valenciaport.com) has ferry lines to the Balearic Islands operated by Balearia (www.balearia.com). Sailings also run to and from Algeria.

By rail. Valencia is linked by rail with the main Spanish and European cities (via Barcelona). Daily trains run to Madrid, Seville, Alicante, Barcelona, Zaragoza and Bilbao. It is possible to reach Valencia from the UK by train with changes at Paris and Barcelona. Spain's train company, RENFE (www.renfe.com) operates three stations in Valencia: **Estación del Norte** (the main one); **Estación del Cabañal**, near the seafront; and **Joaquín Sorolla**, the terminal of the high-speed AVE trains, 800m south of the Estación del Norte.

By car. The region's principal routes – the A7 motorway (toll-free) and the N340 (north) and N332 (south) – run along the coast. The latter two tend to be congested with lorries and they pass through many small towns, making the motorway the best option.

A toll-free motorway, the A3, connects Valencia with Madrid. Other major motorways are the A23 to Teruel and Zaragoza and the A35 (south) motorway to Xàtiva, becoming the A31 to Albacete.

By coach (long-distance bus). Valencia's coach/bus station, the Estación de Autobuses (Avenida Menéndez Pidal, www.alsa.es/estaciones/estacionvalencia), is next door to the Nuevo Centro shopping centre on the north bank of the Turia riverbed. It has coach links with the main Valencian and Spanish cities, and some European cities via Barcelona. From the coach station, you can take a local bus or the metro to the city centre.

Guides and tours

Guided tours. There are guided tours of the historical centre of Valencia in English daily during the summer season (usually 10am; 2hr; prices from €18 per adult). Specialised tours also run to Valencia of the Holy Grail and the Ceramics Museum. For details and bookings visit www.visitvalencia.com. Various operators, including Valencia Guías (www.valenciaguias.com), also offer private tours of the city and its hinterland.

Bus turistic. Departing from the Plaza de la Reina, this tourist bus (www.valenciabusturistic.com) loops around the main sights of the city and out to the seafront, calling at seventeen stops along the route. It also continues to La Albufera. You can hop on and off at any stop, and recorded commentary is in English and other languages. Tickets are valid 24 or 48 hours and start from €22 per adult. They can be bought on the bus or online as well as at tourist information offices.

We'd like an English-speaking guide. **Queremos un guía que hable inglés.**

I need an English interpreter. **Necesito un intérprete de inglés.**

Health and medical care

Residents of the European Union should carry with them the European Health Insurance Card (EHIC), available from post offices and online, which entitles them to free medical treatment (with some exceptions) within the EU. If you are a British citizen who has an existing EHIC card, you can use it until its expiry date. Otherwise, apply for a UK Global Health Insurance Card (UK GHIC) at www.nhs.uk.

Be careful not to overdo the sunbathing, use a high-factor sunscreen and drink plenty of bottled water (*agua mineral*) to avoid dehydration.

If you need a doctor in an emergency, call 112, or visit the **Hospital Universitario La Fe emergency unit** at Avinguda de Fernando Abril Martorell 106, to the south of the city centre, or the **Hospital Clinico Universitario** at Blasco Ibañez 17, which is across the River Turia.

For non-emergencies, visit a pharmacy (*farmacia)*, indicated by a green cross. Pharmacists are trained to give advice on treating common ailments and sometimes can prescribe without consulting a doctor. *Farmacias* are open during normal shopping hours. Out of hours, there is always one designated *farmacia de guardia* open in a neighbourhood: its address will be posted in the window of other *farmacias.*

Where's the nearest (all-night) chemist? **¿Dónde está la farmacia (de guardia) más cercana?**
I need a doctor/dentist. **Necesito un médico/dentista.**
It hurts here. **Me duele aquí.**
an ambulance/hospital **una ambulancia/un hospital**
sunburn **quemadura del sol**
sunstroke **insolación**
a fever **fiebre**
an upset stomach **dolor de estómago**
insect bite **una picadura de insecto**

LGBTQ+ travel

Valencia prides itself on being a tolerant and inclusive city that embraces all. There are a few gay-friendly bars in the Barrio del Carmen district in the city centre and a further handful in Ruzafa. Two sports clubs cater for LGBTQ+ people – Samarucs (www.samarucs.org) and Dracs (dracs.es). In 2026 Valencia hosted the Gay Games XII, the world's largest LGBTQ+ sports and culture event, held every four years. Check the city's tourist website (www.visitvalencia.com) for more information on Valencia's LGBTQ+ scene.

Language

Valencia has two official languages, Valencian (*valenciano*), which is a variant of Catalan, and Spanish, more properly called Castilian (*castellano*, that is, the language of Castile). Both are legally recognised by the Spanish constitution and are used daily. Many street names are in Valencian, and official papers are usually in both languages. This book uses Castilian names by default but where a place is always referred to by its Valencian name, that is what is given.

English **Valencian/Castilian**
good morning/good day **bon dia/buenos días**
good afternoon/good evening **bona tarda/buenas tardes**
goodnight **bona nit/buenas noches**
please **per favor/por favor**
thank you **gràcies/gracias**
you're welcome **de res/de nada**
goodbye **adéu/adiós**

Lost property

If you lose a valuable item, report the loss to the Municipal Police or the Guardia Civíl. Ask for a copy of the police report, which you will need to make an insurance claim once you are home.

I've lost my wallet/handbag/passport/telephone. **He perdido mi cartera/bolso/pasaporte/teléfono.**

Maps

The tourist information office gives out good maps of the city centre. To navigate the outskirts, you may want to buy a more detailed map or use one online. **Regolf** (Calle de la Mar 47, www.libreriaregolf.com) is a specialist cartography shop. If you plan to walk in the countryside, it's best to take a decent map with you so you don't have to rely on an internet signal.

Street names in Valencia may be given in Spanish (Castilian) or in the Valencian language.

English **Valencian/Castilian**
avenue **avinguda/avenida**
street **carrer/calle**
church **església/iglesia**
palace **palau/palacio**
boulevard **passeig/paseo**
square **plaça/plaza**

Money

Currency. The monetary unit of Spain is the euro (€); with one hundred cents making 1 euro. Coins: cents 1, 2, 5, 10, 20 and 50, and euros 1 and 2. Banknotes: euros 5, 10, 20, 50, 100, 200 and 500.

Banking hours. Usually Monday–Friday 8.30am–2.30pm. Only a few branches are open on Saturday mornings. ATMs (*cajeros automáticos*) are readily available across the city, though your bank may charge a handling fee.

Changing money. Banks are the best places to change money. Most hotels will also offer exhange services, albeit at a slightly less favourable rate. Remember to take your passport with you.

Credit/debit cards. Accepted almost everywhere, and contactless payment is standard practice. Spaniards also use direct transfer apps like Bizum and Revolut, which are also convenient for splitting a restaurant bill between friends.

Where's the nearest bank? **¿Dónde está el banco más cercano?**
Where is the nearest cashpoint? **¿Dónde está el cajero más cercano ?**

I want to change some pounds/dollars. **Quiero cambiar libras/dólares.**
Can I pay with this credit card? **¿Puedo pagar con esta tarjeta de crédito?**

Opening times

Shops. Usual opening hours are Monday–Saturday 10am–8.30pm. The big department stores open all day 10am–9/10pm. Shops are closed on Sundays except on special occasions such as the run-up to Christmas.

Government offices and most businesses. Open Monday–Friday 8.30am–2pm (government institutions) and 9am–8pm (companies).

Restaurants. Mealtimes in Spain are later than in the rest of Europe. Breakfast is usually served 7.30–10am; lunch 2–3.30pm; and dinner generally 9–10.30pm.

Museums. Generally, open Tuesday–Saturday 10am–8pm; very few shutter for lunch. Most are closed on Monday.

Entertainment venues. Most cinemas have several showings a day between 4pm and 11pm. Some theatres offer two performances a day at 6pm and 10pm. Pubs and musical venues are generally open 9pm–3am and clubs 11.30pm–5am.

Photography

Wherever possible, ask people for their permission before you take their picture. It is forbidden to take photographs of any military bases, military or naval port areas, police or military personnel.

Police

Valencia has two kinds of police force: the national police (*policía nacional*), dealing with serious crime, and the local police (*policía local*) in charge of public order. Spain has a third force, the civil guard (*guardia civil*), which operates in the countryside and patrols the main roads. In Valencia, dial **092** for the local police and **091** for the national police. The main local police station is at Calle d'Alt 5, a short way north of the Plaza del Tossal.

Where's the nearest police station? **¿Dónde está la comisaría de policía más cercana?**

Public holidays

1 January Año Nuevo
6 January Epifanía (Día de Reyes)
22 January San Vicente Mártir
19 March San José (Las Fallas)
1 May Fiesta del Trabajo
15 August Asunción de Nuestra Señora (Virgen de agosto)
9 October Día de la Comunidad Valenciana
12 October Día de la Hispanidad
1 November Todos los Santos
6 December Día de la Constitución
8 December La Inmaculada Concepción
25 December Navidad
Movable dates:
Late March/April Viernes Santo
Late March/April Lunes de Pascua
Late March/April San Vicente Ferrer

Religion

The national religion of Spain is Roman Catholicism, and mass takes place in almost all the city's churches on Sundays and sometimes on other days. There are also places of worship for other faiths in Valencia: ask the tourist information office for details.

Telephones

Spain's country code is **34**. Valencia's provincial area code for landlines, **96**, must be dialled before all phone numbers, even for local calls.

To make an international call, dial **00** + country code + phone number, omitting the initial zero. The country code for the UK is **44**, for US and Canada **1**, for Australia **61** and for Ireland **353**.

To find a phone number, search www.paginasamarillas.es.

Time zones

Spanish time coincides with that of most of Western Europe: Greenwich Mean Time plus one hour. In spring, clocks are put forward an hour, maintaining the one-hour difference.

New York	London	**Spain**	Sydney	Auckland
6am	11am	**noon**	8pm	10pm

Tipping

A service charge is normally included in hotel and restaurant bills, and tipping is not obligatory, but it is the normal practice to leave a little small change on a bar counter or restaurant table if the service was satisfactory. If you want to tip a taxi driver, five percent will be enough. A common Spanish way of tipping in all circumstances is to round up the bill to the nearest euro or so.

Toilets

There are not many public toilets in Valencia. Usually, the most convenient option is to use those in a department store like El Corte Inglés, or in a bar or café – in the latter cases, it is polite to buy a drink.

In Spanish there are several words for toilets, the most common are *servicios*, *aseos* and *lavabos*.

Tourist information

The main tourist offices for the city are:

Calle de la Paz 48; open Mon–Fri 9am–6pm, Sat 9.30am–5.30pm, Sun 10am–2pm. For information about the city and the whole Valencian region.

Plaza del Ayuntamiento 1; open Mon–Fri 9am–6pm, Sat 9.30am–5.30pm, Sun 10am–2pm.
Estación del Norte (the main railway station).
Airport arrivals hall.
Tourist-Info Beach, next to *Las Arenas* hotel on El Cabanyal beach; open mid-April to mid-Sept 10am–3pm.

For information about places around Valencia you'll need to visit the regional tourist office on Calle Poeta Querol (near the Teatro Principal) or visit www.turisme.dival.es or www.comunitatvalenciana.com.

On the official tourism website www.visitvalencia.com, you can request information via the live chat function, which operates Mon–Fri 9am–6pm and Sat, Sun and public holidays 10am–2pm.

I would like a street plan of the city. **Quisiera un plano de la ciudad.**
I would like to know the opening hours of... **Quisiera saber los horarios de apertura de...**

Transport

Valencia has a fast and reliable public transport network that reaches almost everywhere a visitor would want to go. Fares are quite reasonable, too.
Bus. Valencia's fleet of red buses is operated by EMT (Empresa Municipal de Transportes de Valencia; www.emtvalencia.es). There are 47 regular routes during the day and twelve night ones, marked on maps posted at most bus stops. A single-trip bus ticket costs €1.50, but if you plan to use buses a lot, buy a **Suma 10** rechargeable travelcard (€9), valid for ten trips, from a tobacconist's (*estanco*). Alternatively, the Valencia Tourist Card (see page 124) offers unlimited use of buses and metros within a given period.
Metro and tramway. Valencia's metro network is generally clean, safe and reliable and is the best mode of transport for longer journeys across the city. It is organised into ten routes: lines 1, 2, 3, 5, 7 and 9 run underground; lines 4, 6, 8 and 10 are overground trams. Take care when crossing roads

because approaching trams make little noise.

Line 1: Bétera (north) to Castelló (southwest) via Ángel Guimera.

Line 2: Llíria (northwest) to Torrent Avinguda (south) through the city centre, via Ángel Guimera.

Line 3: the most frequently used line, which runs from Rafelbunyol (north) to the airport (west) via Colón, Xàtiva and Ángel Guimera.

Line 4: Lloma Larga Terramelar, Feria Valencia (the exhibition and trade fair centre) and Mas del Rosari (all north) to Doctor Lluch (east). This line is a modern tramway serving the city's beaches. You are most likely to catch it from Pont de Fusta station.

Line 5: Marítim (near the port) to the airport (west).

Line 6: A tramway linking Tossal del Rei (north) with Marítim (near the port).

Line 7: Torrent (southwest) to Marítim.

Line 8: A short tram line connecting Marítim with Neptú on the seashore

Line 9: Riba-Roja de Turia (west) to Alboraia Peris Aragó (northeast).

Line 10: Alacant (east) to Natzaret (east).

When is the next bus/train for…? **¿A qué hora sale el próximo autobús/tren para…?**
I want a ticket to… **Quiero un billete para…**
What's the fare to…? **¿Cuánto cuesta el billete a …?**
single (one-way) **ida**
return (round-trip) **ida y vuelta**
Where can I get a taxi? **¿Dónde puedo coger un taxi?**

The main interchanges are Empalme, Benimaclet, Colón, Rosas, Marítim and Angel Guimera. Fares are from €1.50 for a single ticket, but if you are in Valencia for more than a day you will probably want to buy a Suma 10 card (see page 139). For more information, visit www.metrovalencia.es.

By taxi. Taxis (always white cars) are everywhere and not too expensive. You can hail one in the street or head to a taxi rank. It may be hard to find one during the peak periods of 8–9pm and 1–2pm. A green light or a *libre*

sign shows that a taxi is available for hire. There are two kinds of tariff: one for daytime (6am–10pm) trips within the urban area; the other for night-time and journeys outside the city limits.

Taxi companies include Radio-Taxi (www.radiotaxivalencia.es) and Tele-Taxi (www.teletaxivalencia.com).

Visas and entry requirements

All visitors, including citizens of all EU countries, the US, Canada, Australia and New Zealand, require a valid passport to enter Spain for a holiday. Your passport should be valid for at least three months beyond the expiry date of your visa.

By the end of 2026, eligible travelers from visa-exempt countries, such as the UK, will need to apply for ETIAS to travel to cities like Valencia. Similar to the ESTA system in the US, this travel authorisation requires an online registration and payment before you travel, and it is valid for three years. A new ETIAS is required if you change your passport.

If you are from South Africa, you should apply in advance for a Schengen visa. If you expect to remain for longer than ninety days, a Spanish consulate or tourist office can advise you of the necessary steps to take.

Websites

www.visitvalencia.com Valencia's official tourist website, in various languages.
www.valencia.es The city hall's site.
www.comunitatvalenciana.com Information on the region, including the Costa Blanca and Costa del Azahar.
www.valencia-cityguide.com A comprehensive city guide and information site on Valencia.
www.spain.info Spain's national tourism website.

Index

MINI
VALENCIA

Second Edition 2026

Editors: Libby Davies and Joanna Reeves
Authors: Nick Inman and Clara Villanueva
Picture Editor: Piotr Kala
Picture Manager: Tom Smyth
Cartography Update: Katie Bennett
Layout: Danielle Titmas
Production Operations Manager: Katie Bennett
Publishing Technology Manager: Rebeka Davies
Head of Publishing: Sarah Clark
Photography Credits: Bigstock 21, 103; Corrie Wingate/Apa Publications 12CR, 12BR 13CB, 14CL, 34, 39, 53, 56, 59, 62, 86, 100; iStock 13T, 14BL, 14BR, 23, 30, 37, 44, 48, 49, 60, 65, 67, 68, 74, 82, 97; Joanbanjo 70; Shutterstock 1, 7, 10, 12TL, 12TR, 12CL, 12BL, 12BR, 13CT, 14T, 16T(all) 18(all), 24, 27, 28, 33, 41, 43, 46, 73, 80, 83, 84, 99, 105, 111; Valencia Tourism 55, 77, 88, 91, 95, 106, 108, 112
Cover Credits: Casa Judía on Calle Castelló
iStock

About the author
Nick Inman (from Yorkshire) and Clara Villanueva (from Valencia) are the authors of numerous travel guides to Spain and France, many of them for Rough Guides, Insight and Berlitz. They like to reveal lesser known aspects of these countries and give insights into local life.

Distribution
UK, Ireland and Europe: Apa Publications (UK) Ltd; mail@roughguides.com
United States and Canada: Two Rivers; ips@ingramcontent.com
Australia and New Zealand: Woodslane; info@woodslane.com.au
Worldwide: Apa Publications (UK) Ltd; mail@roughguides.com

MIX
Paper | Supporting responsible forestry
FSC® C106499

Special Sales, Content Licensing and CoPublishing
Rough Guides can be purchased in bulk quantities at discounted prices. We can create special editions, personalized jackets and corporate imprints tailored to your needs.
mail@roughguides.com
roughguides.com

EU Representative
LOGOS EUROPE, 9 rue Nicolas Poussin, 17000, LA ROCHELLE, France; Contact@logoseurope.eu; +33 (0) 667937378

Printed by Omur in Turkey

ISBN: 9781835294468

This book was produced using **Typefi** automated publishing software.

A catalogue record for this book is available from the British Library

Contact us
Every effort has been made to ensure that this publication is accurate, free from safety risks, and provides accurate information. However, changes and errors are inevitable. The publisher is not responsible for any resulting loss, inconvenience, injury or safety concerns arising from the use of this book. If you notice any errors, outdated information, or potential safety risks, please send your comments with the subject line "Rough Guide Mini Valencia Update" to mail@roughguides.com.